IN THE KINGDOM OF THE LONELY GOD

IN THE KINGDOM OF THE LONELY GOD

REV. ROBERT GRIFFIN, C.S.C.
with a new introduction by Michael Garvey

A Sheed & Ward Book

Rowman & Littlefield Publishers, Inc.
A Member of the Rowman & Littlefield Publishing Group
Lanham • Boulder • New York • Oxford

A SHEED & WARD BOOK

Published in the United States of America
by Rowman & Littlefield Publishers, Inc.

A Member of the Rowman & Littlefield Publishing Group
4501 Forbes Boulevard, Suite 200, Lanham, Maryland 20706
www.rowmanlittlefield.com

PO Box 317
Oxford
OX2 9RU, UK

British Library Cataloguing in Publication Information Available

Library of Congress Cataloging-in-Publication Data

Griffin, Robert, 1925–
In the kingdom of the lonely God / Robert Griffin.
p. cm.
Originally published: New York : Paulist Press, 1973.
ISBN 0-7425-1484-6 (alk. paper) — ISBN 0-7425-1485-4 (pbk. : alk. paper)
1. Griffin, Robert. 2. Catholic Church—United States—Clergy—Biography. I. Title.
BX4705.G6225A3 2003
282'.092—dc21

2002154952

∞™ The paper used in this publication meets the minimum requirements of American National Standard for Information Sciences—Permanence of Paper for Printed Library Materials, ANSI/NISO Z39.48-1992.

I would like to dedicate this collection to the students who have shared insights with me in a third floor room of Keenan Hall, or at five o'clock Mass on Sunday afternoons, or in a rector's or chaplain's office, or in any of the other campus places where friendships were begun with the sons and daughters of St. Mary's and Notre Dame.

Contents

Foreword

I don't know why Father Bob Griffin asked me to write a foreword to his book, *In the Kingdom of the Lonely God*, but I suppose in some sense it is because I preside over the University of Notre Dame which he calls the suburb of the Unreal City (New York) where he engages in unusual pastoral work during vacation periods at the university. As an older priest, brought up a different kind of literature, such as Bernanos' *Diary of a Country Priest*, I am perfectly willing to concede that in a modern context the priesthood is better portrayed as a diary of a city priest who operates both in the Unreal City and its suburb, Notre Dame.

I will have to admit to one and all that Father Bob Griffin is an unusual person. As a university chaplain, he follows a long line of chaplains who have included both my predecessor as president, Father John Cavanaugh, C.S.C., and his predecessor, Father John O'Hara, C.S.C., who was later famous as military ordinary during World War II, bishop of Buffalo, and cardinal archbishop of Philadelphia. There seems to be a tradition here of university chaplains becoming university presidents, as did Fathers O'Hara and Cavanaugh. Father Bob Griffin is certain to quake as he reads these lines.

I think I will get the best picture of Father Bob as he describes himself, "a wound dresser of the spirit." In a day when some priests are leaving the priesthood, I have been impressed by his forthright statement, "During upheavels and cataclysms, in the face of an earthquake and lightning, I have only one basic ambition: to live as a celebrant of eternal commitments made on ordination day amid teardrops and litanies." Later on, he says something which I think speaks of real wisdom in a changing age of a changing Church: "The priest knows he may make a mistake, but error is always a possibility for those who take the risk of caring. Not to take the risks is not to act; and not to act is to risk rebuke from the Lord who taught us the parable of the buried talents." Later on, he says: "The central pressure felt by a priest today is from the tension between the official, traditional postures of the institutional Church and the priest's own pastoral concern for the people of God. I, like others, want to live out the eternal commitments of my ordination day, but I can only do this by loving and serving people—not according to prescribed formulas that seem stale with irrelevance, but with rituals that breathe with concern for the human situation."

This is quite different from the *Diary of a Country Priest*, but in many ways the chapters that follow give us the diary of a city priest who alternates between the city and its suburb, Notre Dame. As one of his priest colleagues here says: "Bob's special touch is that he penetrates to the depths of loneliness and heals it by sharing himself. He is a loving and lovable man. He perceives suffering and loneliness, feels it in himself, articulates it, theologizes about it, and the result is an engrossing meditation on the human condition. The rhythms of grace all around us are the signs of God's presence, His longing to love and be loved."

I have often said that if I had one wish about the University of Notre Dame, I would wish that it might be a place where people cared about each other. I am sure this is true from top to bottom, but it takes very real people like Father Bob Griffin to make it come true for our students. Father Bob is a pastor first and foremost and, despite his enormous size, he is equally at home with the urchins who dance around his altar at the 11:00 A.M. Urchins' Mass on Sunday and with the students who come to his room during the unlikely hours of 1:00 A.M. to 5:00 A.M. to unload their problems in the quiet and darkness of the night.

There is something about this book that is bittersweet because it is the story of people who have touched their loneliness with the loneliness of this huge priest whose heart is as large as his body and whose spirit reaches out to all who suffer and long for healing.

Here and there in this account one might become queasy about Father Bob's expression of theology. He has often said that he is queasy about this himself. As an ex-theologian caught up in twenty-four years of administration, I am not the best of judges in this matter. However, I can say with fullness of conviction that I have no queasiness about the quality of Father Bob's Christlike heart and the way in which it reaches out to the bruised and broken as did the heart of Christ as He walked those lonely paths in Palestine and reached out to everyone who suffered spiritually or physically.

Father Bob will be embarrassed that I have mentioned him in the same sentence with Bernanos because fundamentally he loves literature and recognizes it when it is good. I am sure those who read these pages will recognize the priest in the modern context who may occasionally make a mistake, but always dares to love those who, above all, need love for redemption.

THEODORE M. HESBURGH, C.S.C.
President Emeritus, University of Notre Dame

Preface

For three days I have been living in a basement room—practically unfurnished except for a bed and a chair and the bars on the window—in a rectory on 42nd Street. Outside in the street, the trucks and cars rumble by as though it were moving day for the entire inner city, on its way to an encampment in suburbia. On the sidewalks, there is a steady traffic in human feet as the neighborhood shuffles back and forth between Eighth Avenue and the Hudson River, like crusading children who have lost their directions to the holy places. One does not suppose that these filthy pavements are less blessed than the roads of Nazareth, so one waits, among the noise, to glimpse Christ wandering the streets as a pedestrian. One hopes, amid confusion, to hear Him ringing the doorbell.

In my first hours in the rectory, I kept the window blinds drawn, out of fear that people might stare in. Now, after three days in an empty room, I am willing to be stared at, but raised blinds or not, nobody bothers to turn his head. Yet this very morning, I learned that during my hours of sleep, an old man had night-camped directly outside my window, and only the bars kept him from becoming the roommate of my solitary slumbers.

So, feeling once again the isolation that is the theme of so many of these essays, I have decided to call this little collection *In the Kingdom of the Lonely God*. These essays are, after all, written of New York and Notre Dame—outposts, familiar to me, of the Lonely Kingdom where the lonely children are constantly discovering that they are truly loved.

Introduction

Rev. Robert Griffin, C.S.C., died at 12:30 P.M. Oct. 20, 1999, at Holy Cross House, a nursing home for Holy Cross priests at the University of Notre Dame. He was seventy-four years old and had been in ill health for some time, suffering from diabetes and harassed by well-meaning physicians and anxious friends who begged him to submit to the amputation of an infected toe. His refusal of the surgery undoubtedly accelerated the approach of his death.

One of Notre Dame's most affectionate and affectionately regarded characters, the chain-smoking Father Griffin, invariably accompanied by a golden cocker spaniel named Darby O'Gill, had been a ubiquitous campus presence for three decades and a colorful character on a campus which was anything but colorless.

A native of Portland, Maine, Robert Griffin was raised in a Baptist family, but as a teenager he was drawn to Catholicism by the books and pamphlets of Father John A. O'Brian, a priest who was just then embarking on an eccentric forty-year teaching and writing career at Notre Dame which would in some ways curiously foreshadow Father Griffin's. Received into the Catholic Church when he was nineteen years old, Robert began to study for the priesthood and soon received the nickname "Heavy" from a few uncharitable seminary classmates. It was the sort of teasing this bulky apostle had to endure for most of his life.

He graduated from Notre Dame in 1949 and was ordained a priest in the Eastern Province of the Congregation of Holy Cross in 1954. He received a master's degree in English from Notre Dame in 1957 and did graduate work at Boston University before joining the faculty at Stonehill College where he tried to teach. It was an uncertain launching of his ministry, and, for a variety of reasons—some personal, some institutional, some mysterious—an unhappy one. In any event, he and his students had a miserable time with each other, and by the mid-1960s, an ostensible failure, he was on his way back to Notre Dame, to the same Holy Cross House where he would die thirty-five years later. That, but for the grace of God (and, especially in connection with Robert Griffin, this hackneyed phrase is worth pondering), would have been that.

But precisely then the grace of God had the life of Griffin came into a glorious alignment. He was assigned to the post of assistant rector of Keenan Hall in 1967 and became rector of Keenan in 1969. At Notre Dame in those days, the role of a residence hall rector was not unlike that of the parish priest in an impossibly remote Irish village. It required a man (Notre Dame did not become coeducational until 1972) who was willing to be—tyrannical, indulgent, prayerful, alert, decisive, merciful, anarchic, charitable, shrewd, and playful. Needless to say, it most of all required a man with a well developed and profound sense of the absurd. It was a role in which Robert Griffin had no peers.

His ministry flourished and rapidly expanded beyond Keenan Hall, in recognition of which Father Griffin was appointed in 1974 to the newly created post of University chaplain. He served in that capacity until the health problems which dogged him all his life forced his retirement.

During his Notre Dame career Father Griffin became famous for presiding at a popular "Urchin Mass" for children and their parents on campus. He also hosted a Saturday morning children's radio program on the campus FM station entitled "The Children's Hour." In 1973 he was elected Notre Dame's Senior Class Fellow, an honor which had until then been reserved for nationally prominent people. He founded and presided at a late-night, free café, Darby's Place, in the basement of Notre Dame's La Fortune Student Center. During the 1970s this sanctuary for insomniac, troubled, lonely, or simply curious students was open every night from midnight until 4 A.M. "It is very simple," Father Griffin once explained to a Notre Dame alumni group. "There are just tables and chairs, and they can get coffee and donuts, or something to eat. They come by to talk, they come by to study, they come by to play the piano. For them it is a place where they can come to. For me it is a locus of ministry."

In addition to his ministry at Notre Dame, Father Griffin assisted in St. Joseph's Church in New York's Greenwich Village during vacation periods and spent countless late-night hours befriending, counseling and accompanying the alcoholics, drug addicts, runaways, prostitutes and panhandlers of Times Square. He also wrote a widely read newspaper column in *Our Sunday Visitor*, entitled "Everyday Spirituality," and published two collections of essays, this one and another, entitled "I Never Said I Didn't Love You." The novelist James Carroll's assessment of these was that "Griffin's honest perceptions break down the categories we usually use to keep away from each other. He is priestly, but not clerical; funny but not mocking; holy but not pious. Though he avoids radical rhetoric, he is a man of the people. He remembers, one might even say, the forgotten people. When I forget or am forgotten myself, I hope a Robert Griffin is there."

The media titan Ted Turner once famously denounced Christianity as "a religion for losers." Most of his audience—whether Christian believers or not—took the remark at face value: the fatuous bray of a bored capitalist who fancies himself an iconoclast. But Turner was being unintentionally profound. In fact, a fastidious translation of the fifth chapter of St. Matthew's Gospel might very well include the precise word "losers" among those whom Jesus calls blessed.

Father Griffin relished such paradoxes, these instances of what G. K. Chesterton called "a truth standing on its head," and he celebrated them in his life, ministry and writing.

Griff, as he was called by most of the countless people who came to know and love him, relished a lot of things, including prime rib, Manhattans, club sandwiches, and chocolate chip cookies. His appetite, while fastidious, was prodigious, and his consequent girth was legendary. My first encounter with him, in 1970, was a close one. I was a Notre Dame freshman, on my way to the room of a friend in Keenan Hall, when Griff and I passed each other in the corridor. The operation required me to flatten myself against the corridor wall while Griff squeezed by, politely muttering some pleasantry. Nobody ever knew exactly how much he weighed in his heftiest days, but Father Jim Burtchaell reported in his eulogy for Griff that when heart trouble required him to begin a heroic diet some years later, "he let us know the day he passed 300 lbs. On his way down, which made some suspect that he had passed 400 a few months earlier, without a press communiqué."

As voracious in his reading as in his appetite, Griff loved the works of Charles Dickens, and there was something distinctly Dickensian about this gigantic man who could daily be seen waddling across the Notre Dame campus with a diminutive cocker spaniel orbiting him in comical contrast.

There was also something Dickensian about Griff's writing. His beloved Chesterton might have said of Griff, as he did of Dickens that "the defects of his work are glaring; they hardly need to be detected; they need the less to be emphasized because, unfortunately, he always emphasized them himself. It may be a fault, it is certainly a fact, that he enjoyed writing his worst work as much as his best." Griffin's most maudlin evocations of *The Grinch Who Stole Christmas* or the *Munchkins of Oz* will often lead on to searing observations of human desolation and prayerful meditations on hope and human striving, and there is no dark corner of human experience into which he fears to shine a redeeming, inquisitive light.

It was never easy to distinguish Griff's ministry from his writing, or his life from his ministry, or his writing from his life. He could be very shy, but there was no thought too trivial, intimate, or outrageous to be included in his newspaper columns; he could be crotchety and peevish in his relationships, but no one who approached him for sympathy, encouragement, or simple companionship was ever turned away; he could be redolently sentimental, but few aldermen have been as shrewd about local politics. Griff was not only physically, but also spiritually and imaginatively, a spherical man.

And he was exactly what Ted Turner had in mind when he spoke of losers. If to be a loser is to be an obese, lonely, insecure, nicotine-addicted, and fretful priest who is tenuously employed by a success-fixated institution and perpetually tormented with a gnawing sense that he is living a fatally diminished life, Griff was a loser.

Griff was a loser as Father Damien of Molokai was a leper. He was a priest for the losers and the lost of the campus of Notre Dame and the streets of Manhattan. He knew in his flesh and spirit the agonies of the awkward adolescent, the drug-addled student, the battered whore, the homesick runaway, the embarrassed misfit, the disconsolate solitary and the utter loon. For each of these, he had a warm and ready welcome; in each of these, he sought and served the Loser's Christ; to each of these, he showed the face of the Lord who had found him.

We must beg God to send us more losers like him.

MICHAEL GARVEY

THE PRESIDING CHRISTIAN

Originally, I had intended to become a cowboy, and for the first six years of school, I got booted and spurred every evening in the hours before supper, and I practiced riding a broomstick across the open fields of the little fishing village in Maine where I grew up. Obviously, the demand for cowboys was limited along that rugged coast where the lobsters dance on the incoming tide, and one morning I hung up my stirrups just as I was about to become bow-legged from being too long in the saddle, and I rode the tidal plains no more. A couple of years ago, while visiting a cattle ranch in Arizona, I realized I never would have made it as a cowpoke when a full-blooded stallion buckled at the knees and fainted as I attempted to mount his back. Apparently the poor beastie thought the mountains had collapsed and were falling upon him.

So now, in the middle years of life, as one who has moved from the old corral to the sheepfold, I am serving for a while as a hall rector and university chaplain, and students approach me to ask: "What does a university chaplain do, anyway?"

"Why," I say, trying to look as merely ornamental as a field lily, "he spins not, neither does he toil." Solomon in all his glory could probably have thought up a more inspired answer, but it seems to me that if a kid has to ask what a chaplain does, I am already a failure in that kid's estimate. I refuse to tell him I am a wound-dresser of the spirit, or a professional Christian, or one of the Jesus-people who makes a living from practicing the ethnic of turning the other cheek, because lots of people on campus are also busy with the ancillary chores of the Redemption without the benefit of title as a high priest among the Munchkins.

So, for several years now, I have lived among students as a quaint, stout chap who follows with interest the toilet habits of a mutt named Darby O'Gill, and who is the confidant of moppets and urchins in their games around the altar; a man who is slightly cracked in his affection for candlelight Masses, where he can hide his fleshly immensity, like a shy elephant in search of nightfall, in the deep shadows of the sanctuary.

At heart, of course, I am something more than a Friar Tuck who returns to his room from the dining hall, cheerful and fragrant with the odors of bourbon; under the chaplain's veneer, I have an identity unknown to the animals and children of my playtime, and only half-suspected by the students who demand keys and hot water from me in the rector's office in Keenan Hall. Most simply put, I am a teacher of literature, presently (by choice) unemployed. I have been friends with Moby Dick for years. As a lover of verse, I once got frostbite of the navel from wandering through snowdrifts to pluck a twig from Emily Dickinson's forsythia bush in Amherst, Massachusetts. Most recently, I waited two wintery hours for a glimpse of W. H. Auden returning with mutton chops to his pad at 77 St. Mark's Place in Greenwich Village, and afterward I memorized his telephone number from a New York directory (GR 3-0331). Impeccable credentials these may not be, but in a teacher of literature, they must be admired as sign of sincerity.

I have always had a fear of being stuffy. Given my choice of being a priest who is stuffy or a priest who is wicked, I think I would opt for wickedness, not because it is more fun, but because it is more curable. Prayer and fasting can cast out the demons of lust or avarice, and shabby ethics can be redeemed into godliness by a good retreat. But stuffiness has no antidotes except death, and at its worst, it is more mischievous than Beelzebub in alienating souls from the Savior. As a fat man, I can't afford to be stuffy, because I am always being humiliated by earthy things: torn pants, gaping shirt fronts that play peek-a-boo with my underwear, open zippers, broken fixtures of the sedentary occupations in the bathroom fixture, but you really should know that not all the moments are charismatic, even in the life of a Notre Dame priest. I can't say I don't have my moments of stuffiness as rector of Keenan Hall; but in this role, as in other kinds of confusion, self-laughter can be a sacrament of sanity.

On ordination day, June 5, 1954, I lay face downward in a full-length prostration on the stone floor of the crypt church of the National Shrine in Washington as the Litany of Saints was chanted. When, after ten minutes, the signal finally came to get up and go forward for the bishop's laying on of hands, there was a moist patch on the stone that hinted of weeping. Later, at the kiss of peace, when the bishop greeted the ordinati with the words of Christ, "I call you now not servants, but friends," I wept again, openly and without apology, overwhelmed by the terrible beauty imposed on my life on that day when the eternal priesthood was mine forever.

It has been eighteen years since that day when an ex-Baptist boy lay weeping as a lapsed W.A.S.P. over the joys of Catholic ordination. During that time, I have lived quietly as a graduate student at Notre Dame and in Boston, and taught English literature in the schools of the Eastern Province of Holy Cross. War heroes and piano players have served as president, and the reign of aristocrats flanked the brief years when a peasant pope reigned from the throne of the Fisherman. Wars and bloody revolutions have been fought, cities have died, and the Church itself seems shattered into fragments like a rock crushed under pressure. During upheavals and cataclysms, in the face of earthquake and lightning, I have had only one basic ambition: to live as the celebrant of eternal commitments made on ordination day amid teardrops and litanies.

The priesthood is not a pattern stamped upon metal; it is not a blessing upon a chalice, consecrated to be set aside forever from profane uses. The priesthood is an office to which human beings are called. Ordination, like other sacrament of the Christian life, is an anointing of the energies with grace, so that holiness is imposed upon the profane, and our aliveness in heart and mind bears witness to the reality of the Christ-life in all its human and divine implications.

For me, then, being rector is a function of my priesthood, which itself is a special, or professional, way of being Christian. Being Christian is a grace-filled commitment to love human beings, especially those to whom we have responsibilities, as I do to the students of Keenan Hall. My life on this campus has no meaning, no identity, except in terms of the people to whom I offer my ministry, and that ministry involves fare more than my function as a hall rector.

For some students, I suppose, the Christian-in-residence who calls himself rector is only a nameless flunky down the corridor who passes out room keys. He is a hireling of the university who lends himself to the dark, sinister purposes of the gangsters who run the place. He is not regarded as a man who is prepared to love them as he would his family. When I meet such students, I try not to embarrass them with strong manifestations of friendship. A priest should know his place, even though he is treated like a slum landlord gouging the lifeblood of the poor. With most students, however, warm friendships develop, seemingly on a never-dying basis. They ask you home for the holidays, where their parents can spoil you with manhattans and prime ribs. They bring in their girlfriends, from whom you can get kisses on the pale, withered cheek. In the years to come you can anticipate invitations to preside over weddings and baptisms and family feasts.

Life as a presiding Christian is often an affair of serenity, marked only by one's pain at his failure to comfort or direct students troubled with loneliness or numbed by academic or social defeat. The greatest problems of hall life come not from students drinking (which is controllable), or drugs (which is covert), or promiscuity (which, if it happens, is done without prior consultation with the rector), but from the students' need to know that the administration really likes them. There is the constant need of explaining to students that the university officers are not indifferent to them—that the provost and the dean of students and the bookstore and the cafeteria and the maintenance department are not linked in a conspiracy to sink shafts into human flesh as a way of making the undergraduate suffer. This is not always easy. Sometimes there seems to be an insensitivity above the snowline, and the reasons for the hardships are almost as remote from our understanding as the hiddenness of secrets in the mind of God. Such mystery is the price of life in this bureaucracy whose best servants are not rectors, but computers.

There is another kind of difficulty in the life of a priest serving in a pastoral role—it is the difficulty of being misunderstood. One of the Sunday morning events in the Keenan-Stanford chapel is our weekly celebration of the Urchins' Mass. This is, quite simply, a liturgy planned for the children of the Notre Dame community. The little people of God dance and clap and cheer and whistle and play games of "Let's pretend" as a way of learning the lessons taken from the Bible ("Let's pretend we are sheep laying down in green pastures"). The event has the air at times of a picnic, a football game and a costume party at Halloween. (What does a Mass-celebrant do when a boy computer gets into a shoving match with the sugarplum fairy?) Amid the romper room antics, the Word of God is proclaimed, and the mysteries of Death, Resurrection and Redemption are commemorated as is befitting to a moppet-sized community of believers who worship God in a liturgy that uses elements of the kiddie culture as expressions of their joy and love. The Mass is successful, the parents assure me, in scaling down the mysteries of faith to the learning capacities of the urchins, and in making Jesus relevant to children taking their first faltering steps of belief.

In late February, at the invitation of the alumni, I traveled to Chicago with a couple of dozen students to put on the Urchins' Liturgy for the benefit of the children of the old grads living in the Windy City. The children were simply beautiful, and our experience in celebrating with them made all of us from Notre Dame very happy.

The following week, I received a note from one of the alumni. In a kindly but definite way, he told me that the event, although it had its moving and edifying moments, was not a Mass, but simply a happening in which a priest indulged himself by doing his own thing.

I have a fear of simply doing my own thing and confusing it with worship. I acknowledge that the letter-writer was perhaps right in refusing to accept our game-playing capers as a Mass, although I am always careful to see to it that the essential structure of the Eucharistic service is observed. In the end, after consultation with priests and parents, I feel there are value and validity to the Urchins' Mass which makes it important to a lot of people.

I mention this incident because I think it illustrates the difficulty of many of us here at Notre Dame who serve the university as campus ministers. We are faced with the possibility that a large number of our students will be lost to the service of the Church. For anyone who loves the Church, this loss would be a stunning tragedy for God and man. Therefore, out of a pastoral concern, we accommodate the students in our liturgy, using pop culture and contemporary art forms. This is done not to betray Christianity, but to emphasize its profoundest values, and to try to present Christ as godlike and human so that he can be loved with the entire commitment of a human heart. The work of conversion is essentially an activity of the Holy Spirit, so that the priest works, hopefully, with a dependency on grace needed to mature the seeds of faith which follow from a planting of the Word of God. The priest knows he may make a mistake, but error is always a possibility for those who take the risks of caring. Not to take risks is not to act; and not to act is to risk rebuke from the Lord who taught us the parable of the buried talents.

In my time at Notre Dame, I have frequently offended people whose respect I have very much wanted to have. They have not liked my views on drug-users, the war, sin, redemption or homosexuality. They have disapproved of the shape and structure of my liturgies. They have been scandalized at the things I have spoken and written on the Word of God. I really can't defend myself by saying, "At least, I'm sincere," because sincerity is not good enough.

The central pressure felt by a priest today is from the tension between the official, traditional postures of the institutional Church and the priest's own pastoral concern for the people of God. I, like others, want to live out the eternal commitments of my ordination day, but I can do this only by loving and serving people—not according to prescribed formulas that seem stale with irrelevance, but with rituals that breathe with concern for the human situation.

It sounds stuffy, doesn't it? It sounds as though I didn't really trust God to look after things.

I think it is time for a priest to be humiliated by earthy things.

I think it is time for him to inspect the fixtures of the sedentary occupations in the bathroom.

At night in the Muffin Burger grill next to Jack Dempsey's bar on Broadway, you could see them: the pavement princesses of West 49th Street, practitioners of harlotry in New York City. As a priest of the neighborhood, I was their curate this summer, and my West 49th Street parish of St. Malachy's bordered almost directly on a house of the Magdalenes. So, in the evening I would watch the joy maidens—mostly young, sometimes lovely, always foolish like the virgins of the Lord's parable. Sometimes I would pause mid-muffin to greet them with a nod as they swung onto neighboring stools, hotly panted and booted like gladiators, or I would listen to them speaking among themselves in the salty idiom of the sensuous woman.

But it was as their pastor, not their voyeur, that I watched them, and the Muffin Burger, during their coffee breaks when they took time off from hustling, was the only neutral territory I knew of where I could meet them socially. Only once during the summer did they approach the holy turf of Mother Church: that was a night when the police, as part of their crackdown on prostitution, swept onto the street from both directions in an attempt to arrest the girls who had no place to run. Seeing three of the girls trapped in front of St. Malachy's, I wordlessly opened the rectory door and motioned them in. Wordlessly they trooped onto the sacred premises of sanctuary, where they remained huddled together in silence until the police action was ended; and their sad eyes and false lashes gave them a look like Bambi's.

Without sentimentalizing, I think I rather loved those Muffin Burger moppets. As someone has outrageously remarked, all of us at times these days are playing at the harlots' game, and what the girls are doing on West 49th Street at twenty dollars a trick is not half as bad as what the government is doing at an even higher price in the villages of Vietnam.

Only two blocks away from the Magdalene strip on West 49th Street, at the foot of Fr. Duffy's statue in Time Square, was the Jesus-corner. Here the Jesus-people gathered each evening to sound the drumbeat of salvation. Basically, the group was composed of about twenty youngsters, very attractive and terribly sincere, who wanted to witness to their faith in Christ in the vilest public spot they could think of on earth, namely, Duffy Square; their zeal was not exactly a compliment to the neighborhood. The adult Christians who made up the group were often not so beautiful as the young people. I think especially of the lady, red-faced and masked with hatred, who screamed of her Christ-joy when a black polemicist denied her the promise of the Resurrection. "Lady," he said in a Louie Armstrong kind of voice, "when you die they gonna bury you. They gonna put you in a hole in the ground and throw in the dirt, and you ain't gonna go nowhere because that-is-it!" Listening to her rebuttal set back my own immortal longings to the level of the village atheist's.

The principal preacher of the Jesus-people was a hippie-headed swinger in bells from Sunset Boulevard who grooved on Gospel verses and got more euphoric than a speed freak at the eschatology of 2 Thessalonians. "They call me a freak," he would say, "and it's true: I am a freak . . . but I'm a Jesus-freak. It's Jesus who turns me on better than acid, who gets me higher than booze; it's Jesus who gives me more thrills than all the dirty bookstores and all the dirty shows and all the immoral women in Time Square. For dope don't last, and perverts pass away, but Jesus-freaks live forever! Give God the glory!"

Basically, the preacher was a flower child of fundamentalism, a circuit preacher of revivalism who once seemingly slummed in a place like the East Village, where he was modly tailored at the Velvet Underground. For a while he seemed very sincere, this preacher who allowed himself to be jostled by drunks and fingered by creeps. For a time I was deeply moved by the courage of the sunset Boulevardier who demanded purity from pimps and promised heaven to the hustlers. For whole weeks of the summer I arranged my life so that I could attend the closing moments of the Jesus rally each night, when the Times Square Christians would lift up their hands to the skies above Manhattan in the singing of the Our Father.

In the end the preacher was a great disappointment. Constantly he spoke of the miracles of grace at Duffy Square where he said, the Holy Spirit was working overtime to sanctify the lost sheep of Gotham. For weeks I watched for signs that Jesus had come to the crossroads. If He had come, I think I would have recognized Him, for He and I are not complete strangers. But Jesus did not come, at least not in the way that the preacher said He would. Nobody got higher on Jesus than on acid; people still got their kicks from champagne, and the dirty book stores and dirty shows and immoral women were as busy as ever with the crowds who had been to the Jesus-corner.

One night the preacher mentioned that he thought he should have an immersion service. "Got me some souls to baptize," he said. "Got me about four hundred of them. Gonna have to use the poll over at the Time-Life building to fit them all in." It was then that I knew the preacher was dishonest—sincere perhaps in his preaching, but as dishonest as hell in his statistics. God knows I wanted the preacher to have four hundred converts, but I was sure that they did not exist. I was too much in need of Jesus-freaking myself this summer to be patient with the preacher's fantasy, so after that I decided to look for the God-experience in other parts of the city.

The last night I was in New York, I rode by Duffy Square for a final time. The Jesus-freaks were there, all twenty of them, together with the usual crowd of passers-by hecklers. But the preacher in whose name the work was carried on had disappeared from the scene; possibly he was detained by baptism on Sunset Boulevard. Up on West 49th Street, the Muffin Burger moppets were in full view, casual and sauntering like an army on bivouac, despite the threat of police harassment.

As a farewell gesture to Manhattan, I decided to stop for tea in the grill that is next to Dempsey's. It is a very reassuring feeling to rub shoulders with the working classes.

In the middle of July, I was informed by one of the summer school students that he had taken in a temporary roommate—a nineteen-year-old child-nomad who, from her travelogue, sounded like a daughter of the Wandering Jew. Seemingly a castoff, she was on her way to California where friends waited to offer her love, shelter, and a crack at the American way of life, Haight-Ashbury style. For the moment, she was stranded at Notre Dame, awaiting a grub-stake and a ride to San Francisco.

I had met the gypsy-rover over coffee in the cafeteria on the Fourth of July. Upon introduction, she almost immediately offered to become a Catholic, as though that were a gift of self that would please me most. She was so sadly shabby, so much like the shorn lamb for whom the wind must be tempered, that I might have baptized her on the spot, if I had felt within her any real hunger to share the theological commitments of the pope. However, one hardly accepts conversion as a first condition for friendship. As it was, I tried to make a great deal over the single link that seemed to join our lives: namely, that she helped distribute copies of a summer school publication called *University Forum* in which my own deathless prose was sometimes printed. Our association on that paper wasn't much of a bond of togetherness, but it seemed to be the only one we had. I think I was prepared to love her anyway, because her little weekly chore as paper-girl for the Forum seemed so pathetically lacking in its opportunities for self-fulfillment.

My friendship with this little wanderer never reached the point of dazzling the campus with its intensity. Most of what I knew of her I heard from mutual acquaintances: that she lived in a dorm with a student; that their room was close by the rector's suite; that, eventually, she arranged for a loan and a ride to the Coast. I probably would not have heard this much except that the girl had been noticed by the rector, who gently chided her as a coed who had strayed into the hall after hours. The student who was her sponsor was anxious that his domestic arrangements might not be viewed with suspicion, if the establishment's creatures should discover he had lived for several weeks with this mite of a moppet stretched out nightly at his feet in a sleeping bag. He had called on me, as chaplain, to witness, if an emergency arose, to the honorableness of his intention in watching over the homeless waif.

Both the student and I were greatly relieved when the girl eventually left the university premises. I never accepted the role assigned me without protest, and I did my best to implement alternate arrangements. But runaway children on their way to the Coast are never quick to embrace the change to be bedded down at nightfall in a hall full of nuns.

The kindness of this boy is, I think, illustrative of the sense of compassion that Notre Dame students, even the brutish ones, have for the underdog. Students have a way of attracting stray people whom they can bring home to be looked after by their rectors. Letting them go into the inner city is like sending a child into a yard full of stray kittens and then expecting him to come home alone.

Last year, in the early morning hours of the October moratorium, a group of my own Keenan students appeared in my room with a request that a hippie couple—a pair of young lovers who had drifted onto the campus in search of a happening—be allowed to use the very limited sleeping facilities of a basement lounge-room for the night. October 15th, last year, with its special Masses and candle-lit peace marches, was a deeply religious day, and though I felt like the Grinch Who Stole Christmas, I did not really want this pair of beggars using our practically only hall couch as a crash pad. I also feared the event as one which could earn me a rebuke from the administration. Yet I knew if I refused, a dozen students would question my rights to any authentic claims as a Christian or as a human being. One junior psychology major reminded me of the small wooden cross I was wearing. My refusal of shelter, he implied, would mean I should hang up my symbol of compassion on a rusty nail until the time I felt more like practicing the ways of Jesus. In the end, of course, I succumbed, because I could not resist the mute appeal in a dozen pairs of eyes. The couple stayed the night, and I arranged for their meals, mostly for the reason that I refused to appear as less sensitive to basic human situations than the young idealists who sometimes keep the night-watch with their rector.

Then, last Christmas, there was George, a white man, and his wife, a black woman, and their child, worn on the man's back like an Indian papoose, whom I remember (most certainly incorrectly) as being named Cannabis. They came over from Morrissey Hall, highly recommended by some chaps there as a family authentically in need of help. They had moved down from Michigan, George said, after being troubled by the authorities for alleged possession of narcotics. At Christmas, one cannot turn away a man, woman, and child, if one has religious hangups, without fear of offending the Holy Family. So, with the help of friends and a Sunday Mass collection, I paid rent, bought groceries, and made efforts at the Personnel Office, which eventually resulted in a job for George. But for the rest of the holiday season, every time I dined too well in a restaurant, I felt as though I had offended against the spirit of Christmas and the expectations of the Morrissey Hall gentry in not doing more to relieve the needs of that pathetic little family. Even with the small help I gave, I wondered if I had robbed these simple people of their sense of dignity, especially when they offered to allow me to baptize little Cannabis, as though in receiving help they had given me mortgages on the spiritual life of their infant son.

Simple human kindness, our students can tell you, may not always light candles in the grotto, but it does have its own way of covering a multitude of sins.

Dick appeared in my chaplain's office last year, hippily-jeaned and jacketed, with long, very curly hair, looking like a contemporary arts' festival version of a young, mod Christ. As a youngster who had briefly attended the minor seminary located until 1967 in Holy Cross Hall, he was no stranger to the land of the lineback lotus-eaters, and mutual friends had dragged him onto the Keenan premises for me to gape at as a chap admirably detached from the folk-ways of the Silent Majority. Don't mention Agnew, my friends said, or the Eisenhower grandchild, or he'll toss his alienated cookies all over the rug.

He certainly did not sound like the conventional victim of middle-class morality, but despite the dark warnings, Dick did not spend his visit cutting snippets from Old Glory in the symbol for peace. Instead, he spoke of his life as a student at the University of Michigan, of his draft classification as a conscientious objector, and of his family, and his achievement of being the black sheep among the eleven children of his father and mother.

As an old ex-black sheep of the family myself, I felt drawn in sympathy to this boy who had forfeited his father's pride and drawn lines of care upon his mother's brow because of behavior aberrant to his family's traditions. In the summer after high school, I had sinned against my New England heritage and my upbringing in the sects practicing the Protestant ethic by becoming a Catholic without prior consultation with my parents. My conversion to the errors of Rome may sound as though the Holy Spirit had been doing his homework in the suburbs, but at the time it disgusted my relatives, it was as alienating to friends as though I had become a drunkard, and it almost literally broke my father's heart. He died in December of my first year of college. My final memories of Dad were of our September farewell when he stood alone, weeping, on the station platform in Portland, Maine, waiting for the train to pull out with his son, the Roman Catholic. The next time I saw him was at his funeral, a week before Christmas. My credentials as a black sheep may not be impeccable; but among aunts living in the fishing villages of Maine during the decade of the Forties, libertines and tosspots were more admirable as nephews than were papiolatrists, and I think they would have preferred to see me hanged for sodomy than to hear I was making the Nine First Fridays.

It was his hair that turned his parents off, Dick said. And of course, they thought he dressed like a hippie, and they objected because he wouldn't support Mr. Nixon's war. They told him: If you must look and act like a peace freak, don't bother coming home. So he hadn't bothered going home; he wasn't sure he would ever bother going home again . . . except sometimes, to see his very little brothers and sisters, even if his mother did fear he might corrupt them.

His parents had wanted to be known as the perfect Catholic family; but Dick had told them: "I'm sorry I can't contribute to your image as another Joe and Rose Kennedy," and he sighed as he told me this, as though he were being pressured into a vacation as a martyred president or a slain senator or as a victim of incidents on the bridge at Chippaquiddick.

"If you have eleven children" he said, "the neighbors think you're crazy. So all the kids have to turn out to be the Beautiful People, to prove that the parents are smarter than the neighborhood. But if one of the kids gets out of line, he fouls up the image, and fouled-up images don't win Parents-of-the-year awards from the P.T.A."

I spoke to him of the close relationship that should bind a family together. He said: "Close relationships can't exist if you don't have parents. Us kids never even had a father. We just had a manager to run things, like the head guy down at the A & P."

There was no way to convince this boy who looked so much like an Irish Christ that anybody in the world really loved him. I mentioned Jesus, but he had transferred his allegiances to Buddha. I told him he should find friends; he said that friendship was just a game people played to take advantage of his good nature. I said: "If you're ever in jail, or in sickness or despair, give me a call." He answered: "What's in it for you?" I said: "Forgive your parents," and he said, "Screw them forever."

I tried to tell him of the pain that can lie across the heart for twenty-five years, because death has intervened between a father's forgiveness and a child's rebellion.

"That is why I can never think of my own Dad without sadness," I said, "and sometimes even today, my brother and sister mention the sorrow I brought down on our father's head, because I was too intolerant of my beliefs to be gentle when I told him I was going to become a priest."

"The difference between us," Dick said, "is that you always knew your father loved you."

I have never seen Dick since the afternoon of the conversation; but he wrote me once from Ann Arbor, where, he said, he was going hungry in order to get money to buy records. I thought of sending him a check, but I decide not to. College kids become very cynical when they haven't always known that their fathers love them.

There is a quality in some of us, who were touched in our birth with traces of the Celtic imagination, by which we romanticize the past, fantasize the present, and dream of futures that can never be. Of my own childhood among the fisher-folk of the Maine coast, for example: I am fond of mistakenly remembering myself as a lad with spray-lashed cheeks, warming over wharves bearded with sea-moss in the rockbound villages, or playing like a merboy among the whitecaps, the progeny of rugged skippers who have sailed for two and a half centuries before the mast. Actually, my personal and best known village was the largest city in the state. The last of my clan to follow the sea was a grandfather who retired from his poop deck twenty years before I first sniffed the tuna-infested waters fringing the outer islands of Casco Bay. Except for summers spent on those islands in ancient, ancestral cottages that served as the places for our vacation retreats, my grandfather was my closest link to the sea. I remember how he would take me as a child to Fort Allen Park, in Portland, with its vistas that overlooked the whole bayside. There he would recite Ballad of the Flying Cloud, or tell me of heavy seas encountered off the Grand Banks, where his ship went down and every hand aboard except himself (including his father and his father's five brothers) perished in the storm. Sometimes, with a gleam in his eye as though he were remembering a nightwatch in the waters out from Tunis or spars silvertipped with starlight in shimmer of a Sargasso Sea, he would speak of the shelter that awaited him in the Sailors' Snug Harbor, by which he meant, I supposed, the salvation he hoped for among the Galilean fishermen in heaven.

But my most ambitious and transcendent dreams involve my own sense of place in the discipleship of Jesus Christ. As a priest, one longs to play a role in the Parable of the Good Samaritan who binds up the wounds of the world. Every man is my neighbor; he bears in his flesh, just as I do, the wounds of brigandry; love's anointing is necessary for his healing. The difficulty with many men is that they do not even know they have fallen into the hands of robbers. If they find themselves struck down into the ditches of the Jericho road, they just lie there as though dead. The Samaritan, who is Christ, awaits their cries in vain. Sometimes they perish in their aloneness; and all the while the Samaritan is searching for them, and they don't even know He is near.

I think of the structures through which the work of the priest is done: hearing confessions, for example, in Manhattan churches, during the months of July and August. The experience is like being stoned to death by clods torn out of the dull, dead earth of Nerdsville. Nothing is less exciting than a stale transgression, especially as it is pre-packaged with abstraction for verbal delivery to a confessor: Masses missed, "bad thoughts" indulged in, night-prayers skipped. And the priest, sitting in the stifling darkness, wonders: Does this soul breathe? Is he gentle with love, lifting fledgling birds back into their nest, loving the lost lamb more than all the rest? In despair of knowing, the priest offers the Our Father as a penance, and the dialogue of mercy is ended.

I remember a night in New York when a young Puerto Rican approached me with his anguish on a street corner. He was twenty-four years old, he said, married for seven years, with four children credited to his fatherhood. He did not love his wife, he said, and he had never loved her. But as seventeen-year-old youngsters, they had been found in bed together by her parents. Shotguns had been trotted out, and a marriage performed before a priest, out of deference to her family's sense of outraged honor. After seven years of loveless marriage, he said, he was so filled with hate for his wife's mother that he feared he was on the point of damnation. Could I help him not to be afraid of the anger of God?

I told him that such a marriage was no marriage in the eyes of God or the Church; that if the priest had known the circumstances, he could never have witnessed the exchange of vows; that the marriage courts of the Archdiocese could declare the marriage null and void, and that there is never anger in God, especially with children who have been entangled by foolishness. In the end that young man went off without believing a word I had said, condemned to a temporal hell by his own fears.

And I, with my touch of a Celtic imagination, wept a bitter tear, not out of a sense of a past romanticism or a future fantasy, but out of a sense of immediacy ugly with the failures of now.

According to an ancient story, a man named Nicodemus once came to Jesus by night in search of the way of salvation. The Lord said to him, "You must be born again." It was a good answer, well expressed, I think, and I've repeated it a few times myself. But I wonder how the wisdom of Jesus would have handled the problems of the young Nicodemuses of the Now Generation who come by, either at night or in the early hours of the morning, to knock on an open door and to ask for help with problems that have little to do with the inheritance of mansions in the kingdoms beyond the sky.

What would He have said—what am I to say—to the young heroin addict who comes in, suffering a bloody sweat for the need of a "fix"? All he wants of you is eleven dollars to relieve this night's agony. In the morning, he assures you, he will turn himself over to doctors for therapy and healing. Eleven dollars is a cheap price to pay to receive the anguish of a kid on the near edge of panic as he stands there with his raw nerve ends beginning to twitch, as though he were housing snake pits under the surface of his skin. You ask yourself, is it a real act of friendship and mercy to make purchases in the drug market on this youngster's behalf, in order to stalemate temporarily the horror which threatens to overwhelm the beauty of his young mind and the gentleness of his heart? Or should you insist on his instant attempt at rehabilitation, provided that the rehabilitators will open their shops for business at three o'clock in the morning? Or if they refuse, or he refuses, what then? Should you ring up a constable, send messages to his mother, or lead him, bound and gagged, to the nearest hospital? Maybe you should send him off into the darkness, to beg the eleven dollars at somebody else's door.

"What must I do to be saved?" cried the original Nicodemus. The answer, as it is recorded, is too transcendent to be of daily use.

I remember another time when a fellow came in at three o'clock in the morning. He had dropped acid, he said, at eleven thirty, and now he was having a "bad trip."

He was afraid of losing his hold on reality, of slipping off on a far journey into the inner self where he might be marooned forever, without ticket or passport for the return trip of the mind. So he asked me, as someone he trusted, to talk to him, to keep his mind busy with the ho-hum trivia of the rat race in order to keep his expanding consciousness from foundering among the breakers of illusion. For two and a half hours, I chattered frantically, seemingly his only link with the world called real. Occasionally he interrupted, to tell me the room was swarming with cockroaches, as indeed it may have been, or to indicate that he was viewing the scene in triplicate. Once, he lifted his hands to describe his fingers as tipped with fire, so that they must have appeared to him like burning candelabra semi-circling his head with tiaras of light. But he forbade me to ask questions about his phantasmagoria, lest his detachment from it be destroyed, and I was in no mood to disobey.

At five thirty, his mind was sufficiently in control of itself for him to risk returning to his own hall. I promised I would leave my door unlocked in case I was again needed to prevent his entry into a psychedelic world whose outer beauty, when it appeared without horror, was only a mask, he feared, for the darkness that lies at the heart of life.

This boy was only badly frightened, I am told by the campus initiates in the arcana of drugs. If he had been really tripping badly, they say, he would have lacked the initiative to call for help.

Perhaps so, but during the battle for that boy's mind—as it seemed melodramatically to be—I felt like a midget wrestling with monsters on the last, lonely shore of the prehistoric world. I hoped then never to feel such aloneness again.

But of course I have felt such aloneness since then, and will continue to do so, for there have been other experiences with kids on drugs on this campus, and there will be more this year. No fully accredited human being would not want to be with them if the experience blows up in their face.

Anyway, a priest ordained in celibacy should be an expert in the experience of aloneness, that solitary time of the heart when it seems like it has always been three o'clock in the morning in the depth of the soul.

On February 3rd, 1970, a litter of cocker spaniels was born at the Bijidate Kennel in south Bend, sired by a stud named Dusty and whelped by a dame called Pupper. The runt of the litter, and the only male, was a tiny ball of pedigreed fur afterward known as Darby O'Gill.

On Darby's earliest days, I can tell you nothing except that I first saw him on the 17th of March, St. Patrick's Day, when he was still wobbly in the hind haunches; compared in weight and size to his sisters, he looked as pitiable as a slum-child asleep in the snow. Two weeks later, I brought him home to Keenan. Even then, he weighed only three pounds, and he cost fifty dollars. I had to borrow the fifty from a friend; the debt was later repaid from a gift of money presented to the rector by the Keenan buckaroos at their annual banquet. Originally, I had intended to call the pup Brian Boru, after the great Irish king who, a thousand years ago, swept the invading Danes into the sea. But a New York Irishman, Mike Doran, persuaded me to christen the stout-hearted, floppy-eared mite after Darby O'Gill, the hero of a book of short stories, *Darby O'Gill and the Good People*, which Mike had once fetched home for me from the library.

Of Darby's recent history I would like to mention only the incident last May when a directive thundered forth from the office of the Dean of Students: "Get rid of the dog!" The crux of my eventually successful appeal to Fr. McCarragher was this: Darby O'Gill is important to me not only as the pet to a celibate fearful of loneliness, or as a mascot to hall community of bachelors who, if the choice were given, would rather see an Ali McGraw scampering around their rector's room, nipping at his kneecap, than all the O'Gill's in creation. Darby is important, I said (using the neatly-purloined metaphor, "No dog is an island"), as a bridge between people—principally, between me and the two hundred people I might, for example, meet in an afternoon's walk on the Quad.

As one who is trying to serve this campus as chaplain, I lack aggressiveness in making friendships: I suffer from shyness, and from a social reticence learned in a New England childhood. When I speak, often my voice is too low to be clearly heard, my syllables somersault into spoonerisms, and my speech is slurred by the regional accents of the Down-Easter (a fact my boss once pointed out to me, but I pleaded with him to have the amplifying system in the main church renovated anyway). For all I know, I may even be suffering from a speech-impediment, because the homefolk don't always understand me, either. Moreover, sometimes, when spoken to, an ancient ailment of hearing prevents me from knowing that a friend has passed, or that a stranger has offered his greeting.

On the other hand, a Roman collar is not a guarantee of instant friendship on this campus. Chaps with their dates sometimes speak only grudgingly, or not at all, to a priest, symbol that he is of a religious establishment, corrupt and repressive. Occasionally, I am exposed to the alienation one human being feels for another; one is sometimes disliked, for example, because he is considered too bearded or too hippie, or because it is dimly suspected he is suffering from overweight.

Into these communication-gaps steps my little Darby O'Gill: he is my word of greeting to all of Notre Dame; he is my shelter from the neglects of strangers I do not dare intrude upon. He makes friends with people from whom, of myself, I could not get the time of day; and if I am quick enough to follow up his lead, I am at least able to register the fact that I am more articulate than a stuffed teddy-bear before the little charmer dances off to get his ears scratched by some other turned-off type, perhaps the campus atheist. Doubtlessly, the mop-sized young lecher (in his imagination, alas, the beast is sinning constantly) earns his share of critics, too—for me and for himself—especially when he appears, hungry, unannounced, and without money, at the snack bar or under the supper tables of the dining hall.

It seems weak, perhaps, in a man, to use a dog as an extension of his own personality; actually, the dog has a personality of his own and he thinks of me (I believe) as an extension of himself: someone to answer the phone for him when the children call, or write thank-you notes for bones he receives in the mail.

Last fall, for example, he disappeared from the university for several days. The South Bend Tribune took note of the fact, and the local television station mentioned his departure on the news. Calls came from all over the city, and from as far away as Gary, from Darby-lovers everywhere, and there was weeping, I am told, in the convents of Peoria, Illinois. Even Fr. Hesburgh took time out to inquire—all this disturbance because one little mutt had gone out without his collar on, and was instantly seen and fallen in love with as a derelict, and was taken home as a companion for life by a campus visitor. All my life, practically, I have gone out on this campus without my collar on. Never once have I been taken home as a companion, not even for an evening; and I would dearly love to know when it was that the chairman of the Civil Rights Commission was ever concerned about my whereabouts. I am sure that he has been concerned, of course; I would just like to know when it happened.

Afterward, when Darby reappeared after three days like Jonah from the belly of the fish, some of the Keenan Hall disciples insisted that the Parable of the Prodigal Son be read at the Mass, and Dave Kozeny, the Sunday guitarist, got the little gadabout drunk on Cold Duck at a coming-home party.

Not long ago, Darby O'Gill, son of Pupper and the late Dusty (carried off, last springtime, by the angels to that great kennel beyond the stars), celebrated his natal day by hosting a party of birthday cake and hot chocolate to the children he madly loves at the Urchins' Mass. The only other event planned for the O'Gill nativity is this: the birthday-beast will visit a puppy farm where, it is hoped, he will soon be beginning a family of his own.

On summer evenings when I am in New York City, I enjoy perching myself in an observer's post on a park bench in the Village's Washington Square Park to enjoy the events of that three-ring human circus. Usually at such times, I slip off my Roman collar and appear in shirt sleeves like the rest of the inner city nobs. That way I avoid questions put to me by the purer-in-heart than I: "Father, what are you doing here in this haunt of wickedness?" In answer, I am always tempted to chuckle naughtily, as though this night's pleasure, preferably taken in an opium den, was being financed by mortgages on the parish tabernacle. As a matter of fact, even without the collar I am known by the Bleeker Street regulars as one of the Jesus-people. I have visited too many Third Avenue coffee houses in my Vatican regimentals for it to be otherwise—unforgettably fat, irreproachably chic with my gold-headed walking stick, vertiably a God's little acre in my turned about clerical collar. In the Village, it is only among the tourists that I am unaccredited as a minion of Rome.

It was as a stout man in mufti that I met Michele this summer. She approached me for a cigarette, as Village people are apt to do. At first I was concerned that she might be one of the soiled doves in flight from Eighth Avenue; in turn she hoped, I think, that I was Malcolm Boyd. She was disappointed; I was not, for Michele would have been as out of place with the faded blossoms on Eighth Avenue as I would have been among the Carmelite nuns in the convent at Lisieux. With an older sister, now married in Connecticut, she had come to the village to live as a flower child three summers before. She was now nineteen, and in love with a boy named Brian. They shared a room together on MacDougal Street. Michele was seven months' pregnant with Brian's child.

At this point, Brian appeared in the park with a hamburger he offered to share with Michele and me, but I declined to be a guest at their little family supper. Brian's story was as simple as Michele's: as an orphan, he had run away to the Village at the age of twelve and had grown up with the encouragement of a super-hippie named Galahad, presently in jail for the possession of narcotics. Now, at the age of nineteen, Brian was tempted to re-enter the world outside the Village, but experience had taught him, he felt, that the outside world neither wanted nor needed his kind of membership.

Michele asked if I would bless her unborn child. When I said I would, she placed my hand on the slope of her body swelling with new life, and I prayed that God would love the little mother and her infant with all the gentleness of His triune heart, and that He would protect them more carefully than the sparrows He sometimes lets slip from out of the sky.

I am never good at homilizing on park benches, so I can't brag that eventually I succeeded in handing over to these two park-arabs their passports to Mr. Agnew's America. What made this evening unforgettable was that before I left them, this pair of dropouts asked me to marry them. Not in church, or with nuptial formalities of City Hall, did they wish to be married. Of all love, these two knew with certitude only their love for each other. They wanted to celebrate their at-one-ness as man and woman in a ceremony that would respect them as the alienated souls they felt themselves to be. They wanted imposed on them none of the formalities of a faith they didn't practice or of an establishment they couldn't be involved with.

I explained to them that as a priest, I couldn't perform sacraments except under the circumstances that the Church prescribes, and that in marrying people, I must observe the directives of civil law. As a Christian, however, I said I could witness any commitment in love they might wish to make to one another, and I could ask God to bless their being together, hopefully for the rest of their lives.

So, on a bench in Washington Square Park, with half of Skid Row as attendants, I performed my first hippie wedding. Only, of course, it was not really a wedding at all, I know that, and Mayor Lindsay knows that, and the Cardinal-Archbishop of New York would agree. But for Brian and Michele, despite all my protestations to the contrary, I think it seemed a lot like a wedding, though their opinion doesn't count. After all they're just a couple of kids who dropped out.

Thanksgiving Day with the Glee Club in Boston was spent, innocently enough, close to the center of one of the city's red light districts; at least, so it appears from the amount of illicit commerce in bodies that seems to have gone on at the chippie place where the club members and I, as their chaplain, were registered as lodgers. Chaps wearing Notre Dame blazers, apparently, needed only to appear in the hallways of the hotel; immediately, doors opened and harlots appeared, salty in their solicitations to sex at twenty dollars an encounter. As a footnote to worried mothers, I would like to report that the gentlemen songsters handled the situation with humor, virtue, and a high degree of thrift.

On Thanksgiving night, safe and protected in my Roman collar, I left the hotel, unsolicited then, as at all other times, by the flesh peddlers, thought I was not unaware of the dark ladies with mascaraed eyes who awaited patrons in the bedrooms of the place. Wholesomely, I headed out in the subway for one of the suburbs beyond the Charles, where a little group awaited me, the Family of the Thousand Dollar Christmas.

The Family of the Thousand Dollar Christmas: The phrase sums up that Yuletide just a very few years ago when I was teaching at a small college near Boston; and as a lonely, somewhat desperate man, I had discovered a little family—two girls and a boy—whom I decided to adopt as my own for the holiday season.

The moppets of the family were Loren, aged twelve, and Chris, aged seven. The boy was named Frankie, aged nine. His reputation as a hellion was unmatched by the kids in any other neighborhood on Mount Auburn Street, Cambridge, where he lived as a street arab (during the hours his mother worked) in flight from his grandmother. One heard reports of a father to this little brood; but he was never seen, and he seemed not to care whether his children had food, clothing, shelter, love, or life.

In the year of the Thousand Dollar Christmas, on one of the Saturdays in Advent, I gave the children's mother a wad of bills amounting to nearly four hundred dollars, representing a month's salary and a Christmas bonus to me from the pastor.

"Buy gifts," I said, "and get a tree."

She said, "Why are you doing this?"

"Because," I said after some hesitation, "in the life of the professional bachelors of Christendom, there are hardships to the celibate life never mentioned in the seminary. A grayness of spirit can overtake a man in the middle years of his life, after his parents have slipped into the shadows of death and lingering illness. He feels a hunger for a wife and for kids of his own; without them, his manhood seems incomplete, and he is forever searching for substitutes."

It was a dreary, self-pitying kind of answer, full of excuses for ones self-indulgence in playing the role of Santa Claus, and not especially true. But it was the vague pretext I offered my conscience of the splurge of the Thousand Dollar Christmas. Actually, by December 25th, I had committed more than a thousand dollars on just my own list of gifts to the family, none of the gifts bought with money, all of them a tribute to the fantastic uses one can make of a credit card in a department store like Jordan Marsh.

But, oh! The tree on that Christmas morning: There were dolls, trains, radios, skates, toys and games, clothes, furniture, television sets, a little watch for Loren, a small puppy for Frank, and silver brushes for young Chris' golden hair—and a sack or two of other gifts from the most reckless, most extravagant, most joyous Kris Kringle to appear in New England since Commerce first made the pilgrimage to keel at the Baby's crib.

And Oh! Those months after Christmas, as the bills became due. The mailman with his overdue notices became my worst enemy. The telephone, with its calls from the Jordan Marsh credit department, became more fearsome to me than sirens screaming with accident reports through the winter night.

Finally, the last bill of the Thousand Dollar Christmas was paid. But the embarrassment at my indebtedness has lasted up to now, when, for the first time, I mention my wild spree so publicly that my prodigality will be fully known by a father superior who trusted me to keep my freely-chose commitment to the vow of poverty.

I write of the Thousand Dollar Christmas now, not out of a desire for self-humiliation, for, despite everything, I loved that madcap adventure too much to become a public penitent over it. I write of it because, on Thanksgiving night, on my way to visit that little family, I thought of the prostitutes in that Boston hotel, and of the reasons why a man will give himself a Christmas gift of three young children and their mother, for whom he can decorate a tree with gifts. I know the reasons why I chose the single state; but to me, the essential mystery of a prostitute's life (harlots, like priests, not being particularly known as family makers) is that a woman should have no better use for her sexuality than to sell it for a price on the streets.

So, on Thanksgiving night, I worried about the lollipops who were trying to flirt with the second tenors of the Glee Club in the hotel of our one-night stand. I wondered if any of them had ever needed to spend a Thousand Dollar Christmas with a family of children. If so, I wondered if getting the money to pay off their credit charges had been as painful an experience to them as it had been to me. Somehow, I rather hoped it hadn't.

URCHINS' MASS

For me, the most unforgettable forty-five minutes of the week has been the eleven o'clock hour on Sunday mornings, when I offer the Urchins' Mass in the Keenan-Stanford Chapel. During these brief moments of liturgy, the tensions of the weekend, and of the inner self, drop away; and I can feel the wrinkles of age disappearing, as though my face were the spot where cares have just folded their tents like Arabs. I am faced only with the beauty of children singing, dancing and clapping their hands to celebrate the unseen mysteries of a reality whose own best incarnation, in every generation but Christ's, is themselves.

The Urchins' Mass is attended also, of course, by moppets, and even sometimes by gamins, though the gamin count is pretty low on the Notre Dame campus. Perhaps that is just as well, because gamins sometimes have runny noses, and pinch. Illustrative of gamins, I remember a set of them, twin boys aged five, from the Puerto Rican ghetto of New York City. Both of them would come up to you in the streets and wrap themselves lovingly around your legs. But one was a gentle child, and the other a pincher, and physically, you couldn't tell them apart. You would think you were being caressed by the decent little chap, when all of a sudden he would begin twisting your flesh between his fingernails until you were ready to faint, and you would know you had been foiled again by the little hypocrisies of love. As a result, I am always a little pinch-shy around the gamin-type of kid, which goes to show, I think, that even among us sentimentalists, Golding's novel, *The Lord of the Flies*, was not needed to clue us to the darker side of childhood.

Fortunately, our Notre Dame children are not gamins, and do not pinch, at least not during Mass. They may disease you with mumps or spill wax on the altar linens when they blow out candles at the Offertory; and on one recent Sunday, a child even tossed up his cookies on the rug. But that happened at Sacred Heart Church, where most anyone can suffer from troubled cookies. The child had been invited, along with other youngsters, to stand in the sanctuary for the Canon, and I suppose the little tyke got nervous from being stared at by the advocates of Family Planning. But the urchin-and-moppet set never gets nervous (I hope) in the Keenan-Stanford chapel, because they know (please God, they do) that it is their ball park, and that parents who object to fidgeting in the holy places had better watch themselves, or they'll be sent to the rear of the chapel, where a nun can keep her grim eyes on them.

There are always surprises at the romper room version of the Eucharistic celebration. One Sunday, for example, I was very much surprised to find myself praying for the good health of the Holy Spirit. It happened at that time of the Mass when we were remembering grandparents and families and school chums who were sick. Suddenly, someone offered a petition for God. Then it was suggested that we pray for the world, followed by two prayer requests on behalf of Jesus, and finally the Holy Spirit was mentioned as someone definitely in need of our help. I hadn't realized that the Trinity was in need of outside assistance; but remembering the insight from *Green Pastures* that says that even bein' Gawd ain't no bed of roses, I silently prayed that the Divine Persons might keep a watchful, loving eye on one another. I'm not sure how orthodox that was, but it certainly was as valid as the prayers of one little boy who told me, after Mass, that he had commended Jesus to the safe-keeping of Thidwick, the Big-Hearted Moose.

The chief and continuing delight of the Mass is the children themselves. As they gather close to the altar, I look around to see the fair Eileen, whom I reverence as a semi-mystic of the Eucharist; or little Carl, that towheaded child who chases away the shadows on the dimmest mornings; or tiny Christina, who dances around the sanctuary as though she were modeling as a sunbeam. It was Christina, at Thanksgiving, who gave me the pinecone turkey with the paper feathers and gobbler's head.

I said to her, "I think it is the nicest turkey I have ever seen."

"Yes," she said, "I know it is." It was obvious, as a maker of turkeys, she was not troubled by any false modesty stemming from her amateur status as a bird artist.

Then there are the other children with whom I carry on a running dialogue during the entire service. They check the weight and size of the Eucharistic loaf like a delegation from the Liturgical Commission. They peep into the chalice before the Consecration, as though to make sure that the wine awaits the Lord's coming; and they peek into it afterward, as though hoping that His glory might shine through.

The Canon is a continuing catechesis; and if we find ourselves getting restive we sing a hymn, preferably with our eyes closed, to shut out the distraction that lure us into mischief. Sometimes, we just turn around slowly in circles, in a kind of dance step, or during the Our Father we join hands and move clock-wise around the altar, as a way of converting our excess energies into the worship of our God. But always at the Sign of Peace we become merry, boisterous, uninhibited, and noisy, as though urchinry were racing rampant and moppetry were running amok, until finally the priest has to say, "Enough! Enough!" so that Jesus can come on our tongues to share the gladness that is inside us all.

Off in the corner, there are the music makers: Seamus, self-styled as "the kid with the steel hip," and Wayne, the tenor, looking like a toymaker's version of a surprised beanstalk, who complains every Sunday of the blasphemy of children plucking, during the hymns, at his guitar strings, until he is finally rescued by Johanna, girl sacristan and troubleshooter from Regina Hall. But Wayne knows he gets more attention at the Urchins' Mass than the celebrant himself, and this paragraph is written to remind him that when tenors get too popular, they can be replaced by tape recorders.

In gatherings of two or three, we are told, the Lord gathers us to fellowship with Himself, but He is more charmingly revealed among children than He is by the Holy Name Society. On days when you feel that the church could do without a human element, try celebrating at an Urchins' Sabbath. For it is the moppets and those like them who are heirs of the Kingdom. It is the gamins who will inherit the earth.

In a single file, they seem to come these days; the young men seeking a chaplain's testimony as to their confirmation in the gentle ways of peace. Daily, letters go out to draft boards, filled with insights offered by chaps who have tried to catch glimpses of themselves in childhoods and puberties of non-consummated violence, and who ultimately ground their commitment to pacifism on the ethnic of a village rabbi who was hung upon nails until death. Daily I listen to the young men as they tell me of the peace message of the Gospel figure whom I sometimes fail to understand: the stormy, troubled Galilean teacher whose anger is imaged in metaphors of fire-baths and never-dying worms. It is not until His death that I know Him to be gentle. It is not until he speaks from the cross, "Father, forgive them," that I can understand that His Name is Love. It is there, at that point, that I can commit myself to the non-violent ways: not from an ethic based on an exegesis of words, but from a theology of the Word who revealed the heart of God.

Yet, even as I write the letters in support of the pacifistic young, I am twisted by the paradoxes and contradictions of the efforts to build the kingdom of gentleness on the metaphysical cornerstone of the divine emotions. In all the stories of our religious traditions, God rarely seems to have dealt with man without inflicting cruelty. Job as well as Jesus is a man of sorrows. The pathway from Genesis to Vietnam is strewn with the bleached bones of saints and sinners who have died under the curse of punishment. Religion is more apt to begin with an emotion of fear than of love, and in the end God had to punish Himself in the form of His suffering, servant Son before He could be credible as someone who loves the world.

Recently, I spent Holy Week with the sandbox sophisticates and romper room ingenues of the children's liturgy in the Keenan-Stanford chapel. I read to them, with euphemisms, the story from Genesis: "On that night I shall pass through the land of Egypt and kill every first-born of man and beast. . . . As for you, the blood will be a sign on the houses in which you are: when I see the blood, I will pass over you; the mortal blow will not touch you, when I strike the land of Egypt."

There is a level of violence in the biblical narrative—lambs slaughtered, children done in, and later, Christ's blood split in the sacrifice of the new Passover—that makes the original video adventures of Frank Nitti seem, by contrast, as comforting as the tales of Mrs. Wiggs in her cabbage patch. I hadn't realized how conducive to night-spooks in the nursery the Passion story is until Holy Thursday and Good Friday when I stood among the munchkins, with Bible in hand, explaining the Passover ritual to children whose religious nurture has largely depended on the image of gentle Jesus, meek and mild.

Even for munchkins, the Passover is an event relevant to an understanding of the Last Supper, when the Lord celebrated the feast day with his friends. Moreover, the sacrificial images of the Passover are frequently used in the New Testament as metaphors explaining the crucifixion of Christ. The difficulty is, we really don't want the children to know that the triumph of Israel involved great sorrow in the family life of Egypt. If we must mention death to the munchkins, we don't want them fearing God as a murdering bully who strikes down toddlers as they slumber in their bulrush cradles.

So, in telling the story of the Passover, I covered up for God. I spoke of death not as His punishment but as His enemy from whom He shielded the Hebrew families, and I hoped that no bright little guy would wonder if He couldn't have loved the Egyptian firstborns enough to save them too. As part of the visual setting of the liturgy, we used lamb-shaped cakes bought at a pastry shop, and I hoped that later a knife slicing through the coconut and white frosting would suggest nothing to them of the grisly details of animal slaughter.

As to the crucifixion, all of us adult Catholics have been conditioned to be unrealistic about the events of that brutal Friday; stylized, antiseptic crucifixes, jeweled or lacquered, have taught us to live with the fact of that criminal execution without ever hearing the crunch of iron against bone, or thinking of flesh ripped on rough edges of wood. An adult may speak of the Christ-death to children, but he blurs the details as he does so, and he bribes the young imaginations with the promise of the Easter bunny, before the horror can be faced.

But even as we tailor the Jesus-story, with all its violence, so that it can rank with such child-culture as *The Velveteen Rabbit* and *The Grinch Who Stole Christmas*, we wonder: "Who is this God that we must cover for Him? Why must there be such violence in the life of God with man? Who is this Father who could not spare putting His only Son to the wood of the Cross?"

In creation itself, where God is also revealed, fierceness as well as beauty is shown forth in the life of the world. The earth is not entirely a ballet of birds, and saints devout before the morning sky and sunset. Under the gentle poetry of flowers, there is a level of life that is predatory and cannibal, so that some men have worried about the demonism that seems to lurk at the heart of life, and they wonder if the creator is indifferent to the agonies of a universe that seems to have been formed out of cruelty as much as from love.

In the end, it is always the Easter Christ who speaks the final word: Peace! Peace to the soldier in battle; Peace to the child who dies and the parent who watches; Peace to the tearful, lonely, and aged; Peace to the cold and hungry people; Peace to the widows and orphans; Peace to the restless dead. In the face of all the evidence to the contrary, Peace be to you from God our Father through our Lord Jesus Christ . . .

In a single file, the young men come these days, seeking the gentle ways of peace. In the name of the Paschal Lamb now risen, under the covenant of the Blood of the Lamb, the letters to draft boards are given.

But as we celebrate the Passover in the ghettos of peace, it is still night in the land of Egypt, and there is weeping for the firstborn who have not yet died.

Peace!

As a man without ties, I am constantly on the outlook for a family to whom I can belong, and who can, in turn, belong to me. An old codger needs a familiar chair beside the fireplace; a napkin ring, initialed, awaiting him, with stains from a recent supper fresh on the linen; children climbing up and down his knee, on their way to or from the story hour. Old codgers get—if they are bachelor priests—lots of love and hospitality, and welcome mats stretched, full length, from the hearthstone to the front door.

In the end, none of these family adoptions are fully successful. Parents are shy about trusting their guests with news of the domestic tragedies: pestilence in the nursery, or the latest outbreak of sibling rivalry when Junior tried to flush the baby down the toilet. The instincts of children are too sensitive to strangers to trust the domesticated cleric in those emergencies when pain or heartbreak must be comforted. Bee stings, for example, or prickly heat, will make an instant alien out of the most adorably denimed urchin; approach him with healing, and he will regard you with a horror usually reserved for a spectre at the wedding feast.

Other epiphanies of your status as a stranger on the hearth come when you discover household pets like the goldfish, treating you with the malice of cannibals. I remember one Thanksgiving Day in Jersey when I was playing uncle and Santa Claus to eight loving children. Alphie, the dog, approached (as I thought) for his share of loving, and I suddenly discovered, from his detached posture, that he was peeing in my tossed-off shoe. After two years of living with my own pup, Darby O'Gill, I know that housebroken animals, living among families that they care for and respect, do not make urinals out of the Thom McCan's.

I would have forgiven Alphie his indiscretion except that the next evening, at a posh affair in New Rochelle, another pet insisted on sniffing at the fuming shoe leather until I was afraid I would have to give him the damn thing to marry, and so end, with only one shoe, traveling through the snows of winter.

There are Alphies everywhere guarding the enclaves of family life against crashers. Just as you are about to settle down, snug and secure, as a third parent or an over-sized, elder child, they treat you as impersonally as a fire hydrant, and send you reeling off from the family circle with urine sloshing in your step.

Nevertheless, I am in love with family life; and given my choice—as an orphan rescued from the storm—of homes I would choose to shelter me, I would want to belong to a family I will call the Huntingtons. There are nine children in the family; seven boys and two girls, ranging from ages twenty-six to five. They live in a large, life-filled house in southern Indiana. The older children are married; several are away at school. The parents are archetypal in the spiritual strength and beauty they communicate to the rest of the family.

I met most of the clan in an overnight visit just a few days before Thanksgiving. The second oldest son, a senior at Notre Dame, returned his draft classification card to the government last spring. With graduation coming up in December, the boy will have to face the consequences of his decision very soon. What does one say to a young man—sensitive, intelligent, sincere, committed—faced with exile or prison? I don't know, but I needed to talk with his parents. Thus, my visit.

I remember the dinner table that night: the father, the mother, six children, snowy linen, fresh flowers, roast beef, and silver serving dishes engraved with greetings from the children to their parents on the occasion of a twenty-fifth wedding anniversary. At the conclusion of the meal, in response to a general invitation, Mr. Huntington read the Dr. Seuss saga of the Starbellied Sneetches. Love was a guest at the table that night, and from the way I ate, so was gluttony. But more remarkable than my appetite was the conversation—of football, school, family memories, a Mass homily summarized by an altar boy son—a revelation of the way in which people show concern for one another without self-conscious effort.

Very late that night, there was another remarkable scene: the two sons from college discovering, packed away in a basement room, their favorite stuffed animals from childhood, while their mother sat reading, for the first time, the story of *The Velveteen Rabbit*. This situation as described could seem silly or sentimental, but it wasn't. The sons were just unsophisticated enough to enjoy seeing the battered animals—a dog and a bear—that they had once played with. Someone produced *The Velveteen Rabbit* as a commentary on the life-expectancy of toys, and I became a witness of their journey back to childhood.

The principal thesis of *The Velveteen Rabbit* is this: If a child loves a toy strongly enough, eventually in old age, fallen upon shabby days, the toy will become real. This is how, in the story, the Velveteen Rabbit ended up as a live bunny playing in the lettuce patch. My thought that evening was: *The Velveteen Rabbit* has it wrong; if you love something—or someone—strongly enough, it is you—not the object—who becomes real.

I left the next morning without ever really speaking to the Huntingtons of their son and his future, but there was really nothing I had to tell them. It is my feeling that these parents prepared their son for his decision to live as a peacemaker; it happened so long ago, and at such hidden depths, that even they don't understand the reality which their love created. In some of us there is a touch more of loving than in others of us, and the reason for the difference lies somewhere in our lost childhood.

So, in my search for identity with family life, I hunt for my own lost childhood, and for the gleam of love necessary if any of us is to feel whole and authentic, as a reality that is grounded on God. Heaven is a time when all lost childhoods are recovered; until then, most of us must live with a restless sense of not belonging anywhere, and the news comes like a damp message in the shoe left by the watchdogs of life named Alphie.

Dear Maintenance and Other Minority Groups Opposed to a Rector Sharing His Digs with a Dog:

Darby O'Gill is the name of the little brown and white cocker spaniel that lives with me at 120 Keenan Hall. Sometimes, if you see us puddle-hopping together on the Quad, you may think we are bad friends; that's only because I'm usually raging at the beast with curses and hammering at his hinder-parts with my fists. The reasons for this ungentle treatment are these: to discourage the pup from taking off in an independent search for friends and ice cream, and to promote his loyalty to his A.K.C.-registered leader so that he will not make a fool out of himself over a pair of dimpled, coed ankles that dance toward him on the garden path. The young Master O'Gill has some of the finest character traits known to dogdom; but he has not yet learned that loyalty to the master is a puppy's highest form of service.

But my problem at the moment is not to philosophize on the aberrant behavior of young Darby. Rather, it is now to establish the rights of this little guy to live as a member of the Notre Dame community. I feel he lives a very threatened existence: Maintenance doesn't like him, Security wouldn't die for him (though some of O'Gill's staunchest friends are policemen), and the Dean of Students never sends over doggie bags. Last week, a Darby-watcher phoned to say there were rumors from the power structure suggesting that the animal's days on this campus are numbered. For the rest of the week, every time the door opened, I expected to see the security chief, armed with chair, whip, and a can of Mace, waiting to carry off my pet to a home for orphaned puppies.

One does not want to be sentimental about a dog. One sometimes feels embarrassed over the tender feelings he has for a dog. The time and care I give Darby, I often think could much more profitably be given to a homeless waif. Should I, then, give up Darby O'Gill and send out to an over-populated country for a resident ragamuffin for Keenan Hall? I answer myself: only if the hapless mite could learn to live on puppy chow for seventy-five cents a week; and only if he could learn to shift for himself, with only a red rubber boot as company, on the evenings I dine at Frankie's, and only if he could learn to soil the campus lawns and not the rector's rug, and only if he could be satisfied with occasional baths cadged off students.

Darby and I have grown used to each other's ways. On the days I have money, he eats; otherwise, he goes hungry, unless we can beg cookies from the freshmen. He romps on the Quad, or accommodates nature, early or late in the day, depending on the time I rise. He has little treats from Food Sales in the evening, on the days when I'm not fasting. In turn, every morning and evening, I search out the itchy spots on his ears and tummy, and I scratch them. At night, when he has bad dreams, he knows he can plop down by my bed, and I will let my arm dangle over so that he can lick my hand until his fears are quieted, his heart stops racing, and he can nap quietly once again. It is not an elaborate arrangement, but his little life is in my keeping, and he is the only thing that lives that I can call my own.

I nearly lost him once, after the first nine days of our being together, when he was eight weeks old. As he frisked about in my arms, I accidently dropped him on his head in the driveway. When he lay there on the pavement, as still as a broken toy, I knew the kind of tears that come when sadness touches the places in the heart where one is still a child.

Then, in the late spring, Darby's career as the rector's roommate seemed threatened from above, and for an anxious week, I sheltered him from the news that he might be expelled as a health menace, from the university premises. Later, when I told him his tenancy had been approved by Fr. McCarragher, the vice president of student affairs, and the county health officer, he puddled on the floor in an obscure commentary representing his own kind of insouciance in the face of red tape. But forever after, he has kept an old picture of Father Mac mounted, like Snoopy's Van Gogh, on the walls of his doghouse somewhere under the rector's bed.

After that until recently, I thought that the young runt of his litter could grow up unmolested on Our Lady's quads. But now, dark fears springing from black rumors are feeding my feelings of paranoia on behalf of my pup. Each time Darby and I cross the campus, I can imagine disapproving eyes, watching our prancing upon the turf. I can hear the voices whispering: "The pooch must go."

So, dear Maintenance Department, how does one establish a dog as a permanent fixture on this campus? Must he play football, become Provost, or be elected to the Board of Trustee? How can one gain tenure for his pet, or secure for him a university appointment that will let him grow up as a member of Our Lady's household—at least until such a time that it is decided he needs other children to play with than the buckaroos of Keenan, or until he decides to go off in search of fulfillment as the owner of his own stud farm?

On becoming ordained, one might have expected to plead with Popes, rather than with maintenance departments, for the right to choose a companion for life.

What I really want for Christmas this year is a storefront Church of my very own: a spiritual flophouse on Eighth Avenue full of Spirit-talk and Jesus-bums, with a corner reserved for winos; a skid row motherhouse for nuns in search of relevance; a supply depot for virgins negotiating the price of oil. A storefront church: a Jesus-joint vibrating with the acid beat of salvation rock, with posters of day-glo and night-lights by strobe, and a dancing line of chorus girls tattooed with Bible verses whose kneecaps, read in sequence, will dimple in and out with messages from John 3:16.

It is easy to dream of storefront churches when you have just spent July and August struggling through novena devotions in the churches of the religious establishment in New York City. For the past five summers, I have tried to apostolically confront the nitty gritty of the inner-city street scene where Amazing Grace is just the name given to a sixty-eight-year-old street-walker from the Dixie Hotel. Every time, I end up with the pale piety of those novenas whose impact on the morality of Fun City is as noticeable as the skidmarks of a luna moth colliding with a beam of moonlight. Establishment churches are places where establishment priests perform the redemptive chores of a God whose credentials have been infallibly established forever by the First and Second Vatican Councils.

By choice and by ordination, I am a cleric who functions, sometimes restlessly, in the context of that establishment, but I think that there are other, disestablished sheep about whom Jesus also frets. Most of the sheep of creation, if you really want to know, are off somewhere, probably perishing, outside the sheepfold, while a few aging lambs are blitzing heaven at novenas, with the fathers of the establishment, on the assumption that, if He's teased enough by St. Jude, He's just a God who can't say no. Black sheep were especially numerous around St. Malachy's last summer. Even without the novenas, there wasn't an event on our liturgical calendar as exciting to the neighborhood as the news that a topless shoeshine parlor was to be opened within spitting distance of the church doors. For a while, until the syndicate (that is, the secular establishment for which the city prostitute worked) chased the mavericks out, *sacrament* was a less heady word than *Shinola* on 49th Street, and bootblacks seemed more permanent than prelates in the transitions of urbania.

But life with the establishment was really no patch of thorns at a place like St. Malachy's. I really grooved on that Actors' Chapel with its memories of Valentino's funeral and Fred Allen's wedding, and its thousand tales of Broadway that Winchell never wrote. The table-talk in the rectory was like a gossip sheet out of *Variety*; and the standing order from the boss, when you attended a play, was "Go backstage." The priests of the rectory were on easy terms with the cast members of *Follies*, *No No Nanette*, *Long Day's Journey into Night*, *Waiting for Godot*, and some of the production staff of *Hair*. Dom DeLuise was our neighbor across the street in the Eugene O'Neill Theatre. He and his wife, pale with pregnancy, came over: once to apologize for Dom's mentioning the monsignor's skirmishes with prostitutes on the Carson show, once to arrange for their year-old child to be baptized.

The homily at the evening Mass on Saturdays was always timed so that Fifi D'Orsay could make her seven-thirty curtain at the Winter Garden. When Victor Griffin of *Follies* offered to teach me ballroom steps so that I could dance with the bride's mother at a wedding in Schenectady, I really began to feel that I was twinkle-toeing among the stars of the Broadway firmament.

But St. Malachy's was a parish without children—and I rather missed the children. Practically the only child I remember seeing at Mass was a young boy from the cast of *Waiting for Godot*, and I recall him principally because he and his mother asked me to be their guest at a performance of *Godot*. But no other children ever appeared, though the neighborhoods west of Eighth Avenue were swarming with youngsters too Spanish too identify themselves with life in the neon jungle of the American theatre.

And there were never any young people at St. Malachy's; in the parishes of the establishment in New York City there are practically never young people present anymore. Only on one Sunday do I have any recollection of young adults at Mass: a couple of sixteen-year-old hippies—one of them in overalls, without a shirt—with the just-off-the-raft appearance of Tom Sawyer and Huck Finn, sitting in the very front pew. I was in an evangelical mood that day, and as a climax to my homily, I had undertaken to teach that sedate congregation the words and music of "Jesus Loves Me." Strangely enough, those Christians of the establishment seemed to love that silly old hymn. Afterwards, the raft-urchins visited me in the rectory.

They had come to the city, they said, in search of sexual adventure; on their way to the girlie-palace, they had impulsively decided to stop for Mass; now they wanted to go to confession. Afterward, I was quite sure I hadn't made converts out of this penitential pair, for I suspected that the pit-stop at the girlie palace was not an adventure they had cancelled; but I thought to myself, at least now perhaps it will be a thoughtful kind of frolic, which is as much mileage as I can hope for from one little Methodist hymn. As the lads stepped back into the life of 49th Street, the chap in the Li'l Abner overalls gave me a set of dogtags: one with the peace symbol, the other with the Woodstock dove. I have worn them ever since as a reminder of how two kids whom Jesus loves can look as oddly displaced as river waifs in the House of the Risen Son.

So next summer, it's a storefront church for me . . . a place close to a playground, which chaps will have to pass by on their way back from the girlie-palaces, where deacons will be wearing the dogtags of peace. Hopefully, there will be dancing lessons with the *Follies* cast, and Fifi will attend the matinee Mass. Hopefully, too, the establishment will send its blessings, and monsignor will bring them, fresh from his skirmishes with the 49th Street prostitutes.

One Sunday this summer, because as priest I felt lonely and isolated while offering a Sunday Mass in the vast, empty sanctuary of Sacred Heart Church, I invited the moppets and urchins of the congregations to join me at the altar for the Canon.

Among the children who trooped up to the altar that morning was a dear, young thing named Eileen. She was as fair a child as her lyrically Irish name suggests she should be. She was so pretty, in fact, that a first-grade boy nearly busted a second-grade boy in the nose over who should stand next to the seven-year-old beauty to give her the sign of peace.

At Communion time, as I had said I would, I gave hosts to all the young Christians, and the fair Eileen twinkle-toed her way back to the pew to kneel down beside her mother, who was by now a distraught woman. There had been a mixup, you see: Eileen shouldn't have been given the host; she had never made her First Communion; in fact she didn't have any clear idea what Communion was all about except that it was "a gift from God."

Sad to relate, the host did not behave at all well for a gift from God; it got stuck in her throat, somewhere between the tonsil and the windpipe. One might have hoped that the living presence of Christ would be experienced as something more comfortable than as a damp, sticky paste for a little child to choke upon.

Afterward, speaking to her mother, Eileen announced her rejection of the entire Sacrament called Blessed: "It was awful, and I don't ever want to do it again."

The priest was horrified to learn the news of the instant apostasy of the moppet-child whom he had nourished on the Savior's glory. Within a few hours, he had half the nuns in summer school praying that the fair Eileen would give the sacramental system another chance.

The next day, he sat down with the child to talk of the mystery of love and redemption and God-with-us, and of the immensity of the Trinity tucked into a snowflake of wheat, and afterward the child said she understood. Seemingly, for the child, all the mystery of the presence had been explained.

Then they visited the Keenan-Stanford chapel, where they played a note or two on the organ, identified the Man on the Cross, and peeked into the tabernacle to wonder at the pallor and fragility of the Real Presence of the Lord.

Once again, I offered a fragment of wafer (unconsecrated) to the child, and once again—oh, grief! Despair!—the morsel, infamous in its accidents, refused to behave; and the child, despairing of bread so resistant to swallowing, broke into tears.

She was comforted only by the news that for her next Communion—for her big First Communion that would be marked down by the Church in a great book where people could read about it forever—we would send out to a baker for bread whose only ambition in life was to be allowed to be swallowed as God's gift by little girls like Eileen. And if bread refused to do the trick, I declared, we would turn to wine, and I immediately poured muscatel into a cup where the light danced joyously upon it. Eileen tasted the wine, and she nearly danced too, because she now knew that Jesus could come in Communion, tasting like grapes that have laid in warm fields for long afternoons, ripening in the sun.

I thought of Eileen today, because on Sunday morning she is coming to Mass in the Keenan-Stanford chapel at eleven o'clock for the children of the Notre Dame Family. Hopefully, other children will be there, too—the urchins and moppets of students, faculty and staff. I am anxious that they should be there, for with children standing about the altar, I as a priest can never feel isolated and lonely while offering a Sunday Mass.

Below the theater district on 42nd Street, where the body queens dance and celluloid lovers flicker in the lights and shadows of simulated lust before an audience of dozing winos, there stands the church and rectory of the New York parish of Holy Cross. The buildings are too substantial with brick and mortar to seem like ghosts, but they are too cold and lifeless, like warehouse walls, to lift up the heart with a faith that breathes. Inwardly, the old-fashioned church and the out-of-date rectory look like movie sets where Bing Crosby as Father O'Malley can make a commercial success out of the caroling of gutter-urchins, thereby saving the nuns from the bankers and sending a debt-free pastor on a too-ra loo-ra loo-ra holiday with his sainted Irish mother.

In former times of greatness, Holy Cross Church was the parish of Fighting Father Duffy, whose screen portrayal was played by Pat O'Brien and whose statue is now a pigeon stop in Times Square. During World War II, over twenty-five thousand people crowded the church for the weekly novena services, a disservice to the Catholic piety for which the Nazis were never tried at Nuremburg. Now Holy Cross is a parish of parking lots and porno shops. In a store up the block there is an encampment of gypsies who practice harlotry, it is rumored, in the back rooms. Just down the street there is a cluster of massage parlors, and the advertising posters proclaim an entertainment of Live Male Burlesque.

One day in mid-December I arrived on this inner-city scene: El Gordo, the Fat One, the hammer of God, the laureate of loneliness, the scourge of the demons of smut. For a month, I lived in a basement room that looked out through barred windows on the sidewalk of sin, a closet of charismatic, a Jesus-freak hidden in an enclave of grace just off the pavements of Sodom and Gomorrah. In the beginning, in the days before Christmas, I wanted to advertise the Redemption in the newspapers:

> "To the Flesh Merchants of 42nd Street: You are cordially invited to celebrate the event when, innocent and sinless, the Word became Flesh and dwelt amongst us—Dec. 25."

In the end, I discovered there was more saintliness in the streets than in the rectory, which is not exactly an original insight about any household of priests.

Days on duty at Holy Cross were apt to be busy with calls to anoint the anonymous dead at the Port Authority Bus Terminal and with parlor visits from the local oddballs. There was, for example, the professional virgin of Eighth Avenue, a street spinster of sixty, who dropped by to lament her lost chastity, surrendered within the hour, she said, to a house dick from the Dixie Hotel. It was only after comforting this erstwhile veteran of virginity for a while that I realized her heyday as *virgo intacta* had ended long before I was born, and she was only dreaming of innocence lately lost. I gave her two dollars, hardly a hustler's fee anymore, but it cheered her up considerably and gave me a new respect for the therapy of wealth. There was the other quaint soul who said she was Elizabeth Taylor, daughter of King George VI. Her ovaries, she said, had been stolen by Sammy Davis Jr., whose father is a dinosaur half the size of 42nd Street. Now she needed those ovaries, she said, because she wanted to give birth to a child on June 1st, so could I make Sammy give them back again? On 34th Street, she said, they were turning priests into pigs, and Englishmen into rats for the sake of the fur. It's a lousy way to get a fur coat, she said. I agreed, and then stopped listening, because there is only so much sickness of the mind that I can safely endure.

Then there was Simon, who lived as a beggar at our gate. Every day he would station himself on the church steps and beg alms. He was a nice old man, on speaking terms with the priests of the rectory, all of whom he addressed as Monsignor. Each morning he was at Mass and received Holy Communion. The priests agreed that if you had to have a beggar at the gate, it was nice to have him a practicing Catholic. The rectory was really rather proud of Simon.

Then one evening, a prostitute came to the door. She had something to give the priest, something that she had bought from Simon for two dollars, something he had taken from the church. The priest on duty opened the handkerchief. Inside, wrapped in toilet paper, he found a Host, presumably the Communion Host Simon had received at Mass that morning.

It was not the first time that Christ has been bought or sold on 42nd Street. Others of us have done so, even at Holy Cross, for simony is the ancient sin of the Church. Perhaps this time the Lord did not mind being sold at the church door; perhaps he felt at home in the hands of that beggar with his odd, commercial way of asserting the value of the Sacrament. Perhaps it was His way of saying, "If you are not going to take care of my dear old Simon, then let me be sold on the street at a price cheaper than the wages of a hustler, for one of us must look after the hunger and the clothing of that old man." I really have no way of knowing what private arrangements Simon may have had with the Lord.

As for the prostitute who brought Christ from the street to the rectory, I would like to feel that I had done as much at least once: that sometime I had brought Christ from the rectory to the street in that parish of the parking lots.

Perhaps, if I had noticed, I would have found Him on the street already, only I thought He was a wino asleep at a dirty movie.

On 42nd Street, it is not easy to notice that the Word has made Flesh and dwells among us.

Sometimes, when my thinking becomes imagistically piquant, I worry that somewhere, perhaps in Purgatory, there must be a great scrap heap of lost callings, and that any day now my own vocation, stamped as irrelevant by the underground church, will be tossed onto that pile. I feel this way mostly after I've had two manhattans, and then meet a nun wearing levis and a bumper sticker reading, "Joy is God's/Other Name," who is hustling her way over to the motherhouse for her community's production of *Hair*.

Perhaps it's self pity, but I know I'm not contemporary in any of the essential ways. For example, I don't really believe in the ecumenism that says Billy Graham is as infallible in his faith and his morals as the Pope. I can't accept that pot does more than Milton can to justify God's ways to man. I'm skeptical that a mod Jesus would tell Paul to cool it with the

Colossians, and to update 2 Thessalonians to the tastes of the publishers of *Playboy*.

Being out of it is why summer school is so humiliating to us derelicts of time. Yesterday, a newly hatched cleric came burbling into my office, a priestly infant of a man in his twenty-fifth year of life, so recently ordained that his bouffant was still creased by the Bishop's laying-on of hands. He had spent the morning burning his draft card and mailing the ashes to the Eisenhower widow as a reproach to the military-industrial complex.

He soon discovered I would speak to him only of crop failures in Ethiopia and the domestic strife in the palace of the Dalai Lama, to distract him from learning that age can make eunuchs of our fiercest convictions. Draft card burning at my time of life would attract about as much excitement from the government as Phyllis Diller in the gymnasium in a topless swim suit, unless they mistook her for Albert Schweitzer. At the age of that boy priest, I too might have burned my draft card, but I can't remember. As a clue, however, I do know that the boldest act of resistance of my life was to disobey a sign that said: "Do Not Flush While Train Is Standing in The Station," in Lima, Ohio. I was protesting the neglect of my porter.

There is really no way for me to keep up with the liberal persuasion. Take Mass, for example. Last week it was the "Pizza and beer/Jesus is here" formula among the crowd that swings in Sheboygan. This week, it's back to the traditional bread and wine, but the celebrant stands on his head for the Canon. Next week they'll be using camel fritters and buttermilk, which will be so nauseating that even the Real Presence may get sick and die. After that, it's back to the drawing board for a brand new Blessed Sacrament.

As a old-fashioned Christian, I don't need the new theology to tell me all the ways in which the Lord was human. He may or may not have had trouble keeping His nose tidy as a boy, but who remembers now but His mother? Is it really necessary to the faith-experience for Malcolm Boyd to insist that Jesus had something as human as warts? Does the man suppose the rest of us are of the opinion that God was so nervous at the Incarnation that He left off His own backside? If I were Malcolm Boyd, I would trust people to respect the thoroughness of Omnipotence in arranging the ways for the Word to become Flesh. Then I'd stop spreading rumors about the moral permissiveness of my Redeemer.

It must be obvious that I'll never be invited by the Berrigans to show up with a matchbox at the Catonsville draft board. I'll never be invited to join the Roman Curia, either. I'm just in the middle of the road of a polarized Church, hoofing the pathway to obsolescence. Every morning, I wake up and kiss my dreams of self as charismatic leader goodbye. Then I wait for the dump truck of the Now Generation to cart me and the Baltimore Catechism off to the scrap heap of lost callings.

As a clergyman in the middle years of life, I am used to receiving mail heavy with the emotion of sadness. Last summer, for example, the mother of a Notre Dame student who died of cancer late last September wrote to me the first news of her son's terminal illness, and the memory of that August day will forever be edged with grief. Or sometimes one hears from a priest-friend who writes to say that he is leaving the ministry because of difficulties with his bishop, and you mourn because a chap exquisitely gifted with the touch of healing souls will now be employed as an unsuccessful salesman for a third-rate insurance company.

But there was a special touch of sadness attached to a letter I received recently. It was an anonymous letter, typed on plain stationery from a student who knows me, he said, only from the scribblings I have done this year for *The Observer*. He described himself as one of those people sometimes called "gay" or "queer" (his words, not mine). The boy wrote to tell me of his sense of loneliness and alienation in a world that is mocking, cruel, or contemptuous in its attitude toward the homosexual, and he spoke of his fear of involvement with people who could leave him feeling sick and ashamed with rejection. The most touching quality of the letter was its revelation of the boy's mood of personal worthlessness, which was so deep, he suggested, that only a fear of hell kept him from self-destruction. The mood, hopefully, was a transient one; the letter was written, after all, on a Friday night, and weekends often are times when our most constant companions seem to be the joyless phantoms of our inner tensions. But it seemed obvious that the boy had frequently been distressed by his psychological situation, and that he faced the prospects of many another Friday night when he would feel an inner emptiness as dismal as death. Because I am humanly concerned about this boy—and about all the other beings of whom he is the paradigm—I would like to address the following paragraphs directly to him.

Young letter-writer cloaked in anonymity, I thank you for your words written in anguish, though I have no words to mend the bruised places of your spirit, the broken places of your heart. I hope you will not be offended when the uses I have made of your letter: on a recent Sunday, for example, I read it during the homily at Mass (omitting a few very vague details here and there, to completely conceal your identity) as a document illustrative of the hurt that sometimes makes a nightmare out of life. You would have been touched, I think, by the concern your classmates showed for you; at least fifty people commented on how stirred their emotions were by the things you wrote. A number of chaps and their girls wanted to know what they could do to help. One girl, a very lovely nurse, left me her name and address; she requested that I find some way of contacting you, because she wants to extend her friendship and share spaghetti. These offers were not made, please be assured, out of an overflow of pity, which would humiliate you, but out of a sense of concern by kids who are prepared to accept you with all your goodness and beauty as a human being.

You see, young stranger, some of these kids have also suffered. Everywhere I look, within myself or outside myself, I find that the ground is covered by birds with broken wings. Rarely among the children of this world does one find a human being who is as fully endowed or unblemished as he feels he must be if he is to take to the air and sail the sky and lift himself into the pathway of the sun where the trail of the rainbow begins. But a bird must learn to trust his wings, broken or otherwise, or poets could never sing of feathers fluttering heavenward in a soaring flash of glory on a gray November morn, and mankind would lose the joy of looking up to see a touch of meadow soaring red-breasted against the sky.

In other words, young sir, know your own beauty and use it, if you feel imperfect in some detail, remember that other men are also imperfect. In this flawed, faulty world, the girl with the perfect body is born with a cleft lip, a boy with the soul of an athlete is handicapped with a cripple's foot, a scholar who loves his mind discovers the madness that runs in his family line, the saint with a passion for God is daily teased by the demons of apostasy.

I once heard of a man who sold a flock of homing pigeons to an ornithologist who lived in a town twenty-five miles away. To ground the pigeons in their new hutch, the ornithologist clipped the wings of the birds so that they could not return to their original home. Two weeks later, the first owner looked out his window; there, trudging down the road, were the pigeons, coming back to their natal roost. Unable to fly, the birds had walked over twenty-five miles on sore and bloody feet, to the spot that instinct told them was their own true home. Man's own true home is in the heart of God, and the pathway to the nesting-place is through the lives of other men. Whether on wings, or on tired and bloody feet, we must travel the road of love. Interestingly enough, we do not make the journey alone, but with others as maimed and clipped as ourselves.

Young stranger with the unknown name, I really can't think what to tell you about the choices you must make in the circumstances of a life that leaves you so lonely, but I am sure that somewhere there are special kinds of friends—perhaps the chaps and the girls of whom I spoke—who are prepared to love you and accept you and be concerned about your welfare. But for them to accept you, you must first accept yourself as a being of sensitivity and goodness, wisdom and grace. If at times your wing seems a bit more broken than all the others, remember that the fallen sparrow was infinitely lovable to the One whose image is the gentleness of a Lamb, senselessly slaughtered on a cross of wood.

Until we meet again—in letters or as a special kind of friend—may God bless you.

This is the birthday week for an Old Gent. Monday crowds upon Tuesday, Tuesday waits to hustle Wednesday, Wednesday will have a pushiness all its own, even Thursday will be impatient to die. But when Friday dawns, eager to get into the mad tumble of time toward eternity, the day celebrating my nativity will already have ended, and the Old Gent will be squarely caught on the gray tide of years that stretch midway across the fifth decade of life.

Ask not the exact age, for the candle—count would be awkward. Ten more tapers would be venerable, ten less would be youth, or so it now seems. To be one's own age, next Thursday, is merely shabby.

In the jungles, young men die before twenty; for them it is too late to celebrate the gift of life, and death lights no candles on a cake. Children die at every moment, in hospitals, in the streets, in the ghettos, in the suburbs, in the safety of sheltering arms. In nursing homes, aging guys and dolls feast on the birthday treat, proud to have survived wars and famines, diseases and pestilence; hopeful for more years that will separate them from eternal birth. In sickrooms, well-wishers crowd in on the birthday child, but sometimes death would be greeted more festively; in a relative world, even death and life are not absolutes to be clung to or avoided. For the parents of half-grown children, death is more frightening than a burglar. A father blesses his survival, for he considers birthdays not as landmarks on his own decay, but as the promise of summer following the springtime, when he waits upon the growth of life whose maturing is more important than his own journey into grizzled time.

Even on the shabby side of forty, it is beautiful to be alive. I have been too close to the brink of the other alternatives to be cynical of life and its promises. It seems like indulgence in self-pity to admit that one has suffered: but if you really give a damn, I will tell you. Once, not too long ago, I thought the whole world was a nightmare of pain. Every beauty I knew or cared about lay strewn around like the fragments of a toy a child has loved. Home for me became the city hospitals where an only brother would remain a victim of violence forever, and an only sister shivered in a haunted twilight where the chief language is weeping, and an only mother lived, remote and isolated, in senility.

When best friends who were contemporaries sickened and died until I had made the trip to the cemetery three times between Christmas and Pentecost, and other loses occurred which seemed to totally empty the world of light, I tried to view the horrors as though I had the eyes of a man hanging on a cross. Instead, in a parody of God as the Unmoved Mover, I developed my own metaphysics of disbelief: God as the Unreamed Reamer: He who reams but is not Himself renamed by others.

Fortunately for the blasphemer, there is therapy, and His name is Love. A Father awaits the prodigal's arrival from the far distant country; and for the son who feels more sinned against than sinning, it is almost as though the Father, through His gifts of reconciliation, had fallen upon omnipotent knees and said, "I have offended against Heaven and thee."

So on this birthday, I acknowledge with love the Father who once seemed to waste the substance of my inheritance in riotous dying as He allowed the best creatures I have ever known to be lost to life, beauty, health, and hope.

At this point, the sick are still sick, dead are still buried, and other dear ones have followed them on the path of suffering. Like other Christians, I must forgive God every day of my life, just as He must forgive me, until the time when birthdays are over, and in eternal chattings, the Father can make truth out of eyewash: In heaven more than on earth, love means never having to say you're sorry.

In a world where, within a year, one Notre Dame peacemaker named Tim lies dead, and the other is in jail, and the Calleys live more comfortably than the Berrigans, and Richard sits on Pendragon's throne, and Camelot looks like an inner city slum—on a feast day of the Virgin called the Mother of Sorrow, I celebrate the mystery of birth and the holiness of life.

Happy Birthday, Old Gent!

A PRAYER FOR MENDING

Once in a summer when you were sixteen, you walked with a girl through patches of daisies and wild strawberries in a meadow close to the sea. Her feet were bare, and you wanted to love them because they were innocent and beautiful and full of wonder at the feel of warming, loving earth. Under the New England sky of late July, in a field that stretched to the edge of the continent, you watched her dance as though light were her lover, and she had been stroked with sunbeams. In the glory of the noonday, her head was like a golden chrysanthemum skirmishing with the wind. Bluebirds and butterflies seemed her playmates as you watched, aching with love and desire. Later, at evening, you wept with helplessness, because you were only sixteen and could not own the beauty of a girl with feet stained in strawberry who danced among daisies.

Nearly thirty years later, you remember that day, or like to think you do—but you can't recall if the sea was green or blue, nor whether dimples played hide-and-seek in that face, nor whether her eyes were brown like the wings of a woodthrush. Not knowing makes you skeptical. You think to yourself: it is a fantasy, full of trite images and stale dreams from a sleep, filled with sex play, half-remembered from the awakening years of adolescence.

But in your heart, you know there was a summer of '42 when a girl walked with you in the meadows that lead to the sea. Never mind if it were a dream, for dreams are the reality by which we sometimes need to live.

Faith sometimes seems like a fantasy of love—a half-dream tucked in memory of the years when the Son of God walked from the kingdoms of light, over the path of the rainbow, into our darkness. Touching water, He turned it into wine; touching pain, He turned it into grace; touching death, He turned it into an affair of glory—only we can't believe the dream, because we have no experience of miracles. Instead, we have the fact of the Cross (all of us have experienced crosses) upon which the Son of Man is crucified. God the Father, stern and despotic like a dean of discipline, looks down upon the Cross and sees that His lad is dying. Painfully and punitively, He is dying, with His flesh screwed into agony by the nails and wood. God leans low to look into the face of His Son and to study the suffering, and He sees the lifeblood of His child staining the green of the tree. The bent God hears the words of Jesus, punished like a slave who must be tortured on nails. The gentle absolutions of the Outlaw are like hammers beating on God's heart, pounding away the anger. Hidden in the dark shadows over the Cross, God the Father is redeemed to mercy through the love of His Son, who revealed us men and our suffering to an Omnipotence who didn't know what it is to be human.

In our dreams of God, as in our dreams of golden maidens, we must distinguish fact from fantasy; otherwise we have a theology of wishful thinking, with dogmas from Mother Goose. Is there evidence that God loves me? Does He always scar His lovers with the fire of suffering? Is suffering a proof that there is a loving Providence that guards the victims of the cancer ward, the ghetto, the fire-bombed jungle, the battlefield, the abortion clinic, the street accident, the psycho ward, the children's wing of the hospital? Scripture notes that the

Deity watches with interest as the sparrow falls, but so do well-trained ornithologists. Is there compassion in the curious glance of the cosmic bird watcher, and does He sometimes lift the dead feathers on His fingertips and send them beating like oars against a sea of light until they have again found the wind currents to the sun?

Faith, writes St. Paul, is the substance of things hoped for, the evidence of things unseen. Of Cardinal Newman, it is written that as a child he hoped that the *Arabian Nights* might be true; and that, as a man, he found magic even more moving than the tales of Scheherazade in the myth of the eternal priesthood.

As a priest who serves as chaplain to a university, I often create fantasies about God, writing of Him, for example, as a lonely God who lives by Himself in an empty mansion, with only hired servants to keep Him company. It is easier to love a God who is as moody with loneliness as a widowed grandfather than it is to have to forgive him for being blissfully happy when He should be brooding over the broken bones of babies. Fantasies are what you indulge in, sometimes, if you are a priest, witnessing to the truth of things unseen, like the love that lies hidden in the mystery of suffering.

In the end, like Newman, I am a minister of the eternal priesthood. I am part of the myth that proclaims the wonders of Incarnation and Redemption, and Sacraments that reveal Christ under the gestures and words of ritual. I must proclaim the Good News of the Lord without dependency on miracles or magic or fantasy. I must teach the disciplines of love to a generation that often confuses love with romance, which is only love's foreshadowing. Love sometimes walks in a meadow and is holy, as sixteen-year-olds can tell you; but in its profoundest implications, it is an affair of sacrifice and crucifixion, and only faith can say with certainty whether God is watching the struggle against the nails.

I must teach the doctrine of the forgiveness of sins, without sentimentalizing either the sin or the sinner. The whole bloody crowd of us are murderers, adulterers, abortionists, sodomists, liars, thieves, and other ugly types. The Gospel images of prodigal sons and lost sheep do not apply if used by sentimentalists—so I am warned by my critics. Often, I do not understand God, and I really hesitate to like Him; but I trust the experience of Christ who gave Him His whole being until the ultimate surrender in death. There was such a trust of the Father in Jesus as He hung on the Cross that I can really believe that God is as compassionate as that wonderful old man in the parable who watched the roads till his youngest boy came home in shabbiness from the harlots' house, when his dad ran to greet him with the embraces of love.

Here, then, is the faith—in God and Christ and the Holy Spirit—with its complexities and ambiguities, with its light and shadows, that I am trying to share. The wonder of it to me is not that I witness to it badly, through imperfect liturgies and a theology of the imagination, but why I try to witness to it at all.

At my age, my pores are too brittle to sport in the meadow with Elvira Madigan. But as long as the heart can sing and the mind can wonder, then faith is always like a young girl gathering sunlight: elusive, pertinacious, saucy, beautiful, and full of love. At its best, my faith reflects the qualities—doubt, fear, passion, intensity, trust, courage, hope, grief—that are preoccupying the students, children, colleagues, and friends of the Notre Dame community. For as a Christian, I am here not only to witness to faith, but also to find it incarnate in heartbeats that dance to the rhythms of grace.

Somehow, I had thought I knew what the scene of a Pentecostal meeting would be like from the memories of certain Protestant sects in my New England childhood: Christians of the clapboard churches, professing a deeper walk with God through shouted hallelujahs and Bible-thumping; the ecstasy of believers soul-raped by Jesus and caught up to the celestial (and diaphanous) bosom of Spirit, who spins pinwheels of fire in the senses. I thought I was familiar with the idiom of the charismatically renewed: "Unto Jesus be the glory, brother. Are you washed in the Blood of the Lamb?" I thought I could tell you of the bibliolatry, the fundamentalist reading of the promises of the Word which, in an ultimate progression, leads straight to the tents of the faith-healers where itinerant preachers have danced with serpents. Finally, I thought I would recognize the disinherited children of the earth whose only identity comes from the leases they claim to hold on the mansions of glory.

It was from this sense of a religious experience *déjà vu* that I resisted attending a gathering of the Pentecostalists until recently, when I went to their afternoon Mass. I entered the chapel of Jesus Christ Superstar, wet from the heavy rain of a downpour. I was out of sorts with a universe whose weather had conspired to build a moat of ice and water around my front door. Moreover, I was nearly mortally offended because the Mass was, or seemed, fifteen, or twenty minutes late in beginning, and I was offended by the sight of a stout lady who dashed from one encounter group to another, asking, "has anybody here seen the Lectionary?" Apparently nobody there had seen the Lectionary, because the damned thing never did appear, and the Jerusalem Bible was used instead, which struck me as a bush-league way of running a religion, the Holy Spirit's or anybody else's. I was also depressed to notice that all those I recognized as regular Pentecostals looked as though they were in need of a good meal. I myself am never in need of a good meal, a fact I have always considered as one of the consolations of religion. I thought to myself, I can't really be expected to respect a faith that forever afterward will be identified with winter rain, late beginnings, purloined lectionaries, and malnutrition. At that point, the guitarist struck up a hymn: "There is a Balm in Gilead."

Of the Mass, one of the most beautiful I have ever attended, I will mention only the meditation periods: one, after the reading of the Gospel; the other, just prior to the Blessing and Dismissal. I have never been so conscious of the spirit of faith praying, singing, laughing, brooding, not even in convents of contemplative nuns, as I was among that group of young people assembled to celebrate the Eucharist without their Lectionary. Every now and again, among that hushed group would come a noise like that of a wind beginning to blow through the branches of a tree: quickly the noise would intensify into a roar, as though that wind had passed from the one tree into a whole forest of branches; then, almost as quickly, all the commotion would die away, and the group would be hushed again. Without question or surprise, I judged that the Holy Spirit had passed, playing over the group like a hand touching the notes of a piano.

Evidence of the things unseen rarely means much to anyone but the person to whom the clue is given, and religious experience can never be claimed as objective (though Lazarus, if pericopes be true, might argue the point), even though they leave you as deeply moved and on the point of tears as I was on that afternoon, when I witnessed the experience, seemingly, of a young Christian singing (in the Pentecostal way, with the Paraclete as his choirmaster) in Hebraic tongues. Of course I am moved to tears rather easily; the final moments of *Love Story*, for example, that movie that Judith Crist, in *New York* magazine, described (out of deference to the favorite noun, verb, and expletive of the McGraw broad) as "Camille with bullshit," left me in so sodden a condition that all the salt was washed away from my bag of popcorn. But *Love Story* caught at the throat not from its own intensity, but out of a sadness it evoked from personal memories of my own past. But it was presently, contemporaneously moving to hear the Presence of God proclaimed at Mass in an honest emotional way. I do not know the source, in nature or in supernature, of how it is that tongues are set to dancing to the charismatic tunes of language; but the moments when it happened seem God-touched and full of grace.

Perhaps, for some of us, the liturgy has lost its power to stir us very deeply. Our worship consists in priests, clunking like Radio City stagehands around the sanctuary, acting out the charades of grace without mystery; ministers of eternity speaking the imperishable truths of redemption in a textural rhetoric powerless to lift itself heavenward, from altar tables (still, after more than five years, the janitor's temporary masterpiece) unworthy to be used at picnics, much less to serve at the Supper of the Lord. Only rarely do the lessons instruct us as a people whose past includes the lost children of Hiroshima and the war dead from the ghettos, whose present is the agony of cities crucified against a poisoned sky, and whose tomorrow seems threatened by the death of the world.

A few years ago, after the public funerals of the Kennedys and Martin Luther King Jr., some of the commentators pointed out the absence of "soul" in the Roman Catholic service. It seems to me, for once at least, that I found soul in that liturgy of the Pentecostal group. Perhaps I never will, or never could, find it there again; only future visits will reveal the possibilities of my personal charismatic renewal through the ministry of the Spirit-group. But it is clear to me as a believing son of the Church that our prophets and poets, our sages and saints, have a work of love to perform, a chore of liturgy to be shaped, if the spirit of contemporary man is going to be served in all its deepest needs in our communal celebrations of salvific Love.

It seems only right that a chap, occasionally at least, should be stirred at least as deeply by Mass as some of us were when we watched that soap opera described as "Camille with bullshit."

It seems to me that the background music appropriate to this tale depicting the further adventures of the Jesus-worker in the Naked City might well be the theme from *Midnight Cowboy*. Yet what follows is not the story of a Times Square hustler; it is only an incident involving an old man, a figure sketched in sadness, who may have been (though I doubt it) a complete stranger to the world of 42nd Street. In my role, I certainly was no Dustin Hoffman-like character; yet, like Ratso of the shuffling foot, I am sometimes a psychic cripple when I think of New York, especially when I remember the night scenes of Manhattan: the sidewalks caked with scum and grime and otherwise cluttered by human garbage; the trains that thunder in darkness through tunnels walled with stone, grooved with steel, and utterly alien to anything that is human or anything that breathes except rats; the shops that peddle flesh; the solicitations to share a bed with the hollow-eyed women who wait in the shadows of the doorways along Eighth Avenue.

The incident happened during a recent summer on a Sunday evening, when the chores of the Lord's day were done, and I was dining in a deli in one of the neighborhoods below 14th Street. The counterman had carved me slices of beef and arranged them on a roll; and having set my supper on one of the empty tables of the joint, I had popped through the doorway leading to an adjoining bar where I placed an order for a 65¢ manhattan. On returning with my drink to the table, I saw him: a white-haired gentleman, about sixty-five, impeccably dressed, and very drunk. Except for his drunkenness, he could have been a senior partner at Tiffany's, or a visiting professor of humanities at NYU, or an associate in the ministry with Norman Vincent Peale. In appearance, he was a beautiful old man, and I dimly wondered if he were a recent widower mourning the death of his wife with booze.

As sometimes happens, he noticed the Roman collar and came over to ask if he could buy me a drink. I refused, since he was drunk. He went away; and there, I thought, was an end to the matter.

But afterward, I saw him outside, trying to board an uptown bus. I watched while the driver waved him off the steps of the vehicle, into a street heavy with traffic, and I decided the old gentleman, probably somebody's grandfather, was in need of my help. Rescuing drunks from traffic is an old hang-up of mine. As a young cleric, I once gave absolution to a drunk who lay dead as an accident victim in the streets of Boston, and I would never recommend that kind of situation to anyone as a way of priestly fulfillment. It seems to me I have spent half my time since ordination dragging alcoholics from near-brushes with disaster under the wheels that screech to a halt on crowded city streets.

I said to him words like these: "Old timer and senior citizen, sir, can I take you where you want to go?"

He looked at me, his eyes lit up, and delight danced in every corner of his face. In a reply that was almost a squeak, he said emphatically, "Ye-ess!," and somehow he made three syllables of the word. He linked his arm in mine and we began walking (seemingly, the symbols of venerability with a bag on, and naivete waddling like a duck) down the street, around the corner, and down Fifth Avenue to his apartment in one of the posh buildings near the Washington Mews.

It only took about three minutes of interlocking arms for me to suspect that I was dealing with an old man not nearly as drunk as he had appeared, who was wicked in ways that could only make me nervous. My worst fears were confirmed, in the fourth minute of our five-minute jaunt, when he turned to whistle after three young servicemen who passed us on the sidewalk.

In the meantime, he told me something of himself: he was a graduate of an Eastern college; he lived with his sister, and worked as a freelance writer for the slick magazines. A week before, he said, two young thugs had followed him up to his apartment, where they had beaten and robbed him. However, I seemed like a decent fellow, for a priest, though, he said, he regarded me as rather fat. Since his sister was away, and though the apartment was a mess, wouldn't I come up to his place for a drink?

In turn, I told him I was from Notre Dame, Our Mother and I agreed that yes, I was terribly fat, and getting fatter by the minute. I said I couldn't stand messy apartments, and that I couldn't possibly have a drink with him because even now, the concerned Monsignor was scanning the streets from the rectory door, anxious for his curate to come home for a game of checkers.

In the final scene of this absurb little drama, when I had finally pried my arm loose from a grip like that of a widow standing at a gravesite, looking for the first time into the face of loneliness, this pathetic old man with the face of a saint suddenly embraced me, and touched me with a gentle gesture on the cheek. Then he turned, and practically ran to the door of his apartment house, where he let himself in with a key.

It is tasteless, perhaps, to tell this story, but it is part of the dirge of man's isolation in the heart of the Unreal City, of which, as I have said before, Notre Dame seems only a suburb. At the time, I was angry and embarrassed at the old man's behavior with a priest who never knew enough not to talk to strangers. Since them, I have learned to live in tenderness with the memory of that aging lush who, it appears, wanted to play the role of Midnight Cowboy; because in that final gesture, when he touched me on the cheek, I think he revealed his heart in all its wistful human desperation.

I remember a sad, pre-dawn hour close to four o'clock one springtime when, in a quaint, ancient café off the Grand Place in Brussels, I sat in expatriated isolation sipping coffee and thinking home-thoughts from abroad. At the bar, Belgians were chatting in French idioms, and ironically enough, the radio played a Jackie Gleason arrangement of "The World Is Waiting for the Sunrise." Around the city, members of the Glee Club with whom I was traveling were respectably asleep in beds provided by families of the American community in Brussels; and for several hours that night, expresso was my only earthly comfort in the face of homesickness until finally, when the café closed at half-past four, I returned to an empty rectory for a two-hour nap before traveling in Europe again.

I mention the incident only to point out that one does not have to be an aging geriatrics case out of a Hemingway story to have need for a clean, well-lighted place for the night. Unlike Hemingway's old man, I can say the Our Father trustingly, and have no fear that nada, or nothingness, lurks at the heart of life. A full and viable faith assures me that no empty spaces between the stars can threaten life with metaphysical anguish, and I can discover no antarctic landscapes of the soul from which God seems to have departed. Nevertheless, I admit that I am constantly in need of the sight and sounds of people whom I love.

The Belgian vigil I kept with the coffee cups was typical of a summer when my need for people reached the proportions of a crisis. The after-dinner companions of a New York priest (Manhattan being my parish during July–August) are his phone, his radio, his television, and his books. For me, frequently, these comforts were not enough; and in the hours of the evening after the last Rockette had kicked herself off stage and into the wings, and the Broadway babies had said goodnight to the last rookie cop on 42nd Street, I searched for the clean, well-lighted places of New York where the city never sleeps. At two or three o'clock in the morning I would haunt a bar or a coffee shop, listening in on conversations I was never invited to join, matching drinks with people I seldom desired to get involved with, because in New York involvement with strangers can mean trouble. Sometimes I would drop quarters into a jukebox and listen to Andy Williams sing the blues until the joint closed, or it was time to go back to the rectory to prepare for saying the early Mass of the morning. But it was not only for me, that summer, that loneliness was a problem.

In Europe, in every city and town we visited, I noticed a little old lady with a crocheted cap passing by: stooped, gray, carrying a shopping bag, with great wrinkles in her stockings, and shoes that looked like bedroom slippers. Sometimes I would glimpse her on the street; sometimes I would see her at prayer in a cathedral; once I saw her picking through a trash heap in Paris, and once, finally, she sat next to me in the Penn Station in New York. I watched her trying to sleep, her feet modestly together and her head resting against hands twisted protectively around the handles of the shopping bag. When I saw, with horror, that her legs, under her stockings, were wrapped with bandages, I realized how far the journey had been from Paris and Amsterdam, from Munich and Rome. Worst horror of all, I realized she had no place to sleep, nowhere to go, except maybe to another city, another bench, perhaps in Chicago. Not knowing what else to do, I slipped a little money into her bag, and hurried off for the train to Boston.

New York City is filled with little old ladies who carry shopping bags. They live in the streets and sleep in subways, on park benches, or in doorways. They are the ultimate victims of loneliness, these old ladies for whom the clean, well-lighted places do not exist. Nearly as bad off are the aged folks who live in the cheap hotels and lodging houses around Broadway. Some of them whom I met this summer while on Communion calls were over eighty years old; they were sick and afraid, unable ever to leave their own premises because of weakness and fear. Ultimately most of them will die with no one but the priest to mourn at their funerals.

I was lonely enough that summer, but mine was not the ultimate loneliness of the folk whom life has passed by.

When I returned to Notre Dame campus a few weeks later, I came home to be among young people who are trying, amid the loneliness of institutional life, to create clean, well-lighted places as shelters against the night. At twenty, as at eighty, human beings can, and do, suffer from a crisis of alienation. At Notre Dame, chaps and their girls—many of whom tend, like aging chaplains, to be night people—have a need for groups they can identify with during times of stress: a community of friends among whom they can talk, and sing, and share a drink, and speak of love. During the past year, in my own room, I have seen this happen: kids needing the warmth of togetherness keeping night watch with each other until sunrise. Some nights I have gone to bed, and hours later I have gotten up to find the whole group huddled together, asleep on the rug, children who have kept each other safe through the time of darkness.

Regulations that do not adequately realize the tendency to close, communal life among young people are not terribly sensitive. That is why, hopefully, trustees who themselves know the experience of loneliness will help in the building of clean, well-lighted places in the dormitories of Notre Dame.

One day soon, hopefully, some jet-age Aquinas will assemble a textbook of dogmas to be entitled *The Theology of a Lonely God*. Actually, the traditional notion of a complacent, all-sufficing Deity of Three Persons, needing for perfection just the company of the Others, like the angles of a triangle, is not very comforting. Even a good bridge game requires more than three partners. I prefer to think of creation as having occurred at a bleak moment in the lifetime of Omnipotence when Being God Just Wasn't Enough; and even with the teamwork of a Trinity, it took Him six days of shaping galaxies and firmaments, puppy dogs and infant boy-childs, and daughters of rare strength and beauty, before contentment over His handiwork could drive off the moodiness of a Father with the instincts of a cosmic Carpenter.

As a cure for loneliness, begetting—whether of galaxies or dynasties—helps only for a little while, as any parent can tell you. Even an Incarnation (possible only if you are God) doesn't seem to help much except for brief moments like at a Last Supper. The agape of an Upper Room ends in a Garden of abandonment, and Friday's Cross is always solitary.

Metaphysics, arguing from the interplay of cause with effect, establishes analogies between heaven and earth: from the loneliness of man one can reason to the paradigm of Life Triunally isolated in the kingdoms above the snow-line. Needed as relevant by contemporary exiles: a Summa Theologica of the Lonely God.

Last spring, a letter arrived in the Sunday morning mail from a student who described himself as a homosexual. It was an anonymous letter, full of loneliness and suffering, which I tried to answer. Twice since then other letters have arrived from this boy, each of them filled with cries of help like those of a victim of brigands on the Jericho road. All other efforts to reach him having failed—letters sent to inadequate addresses, for example, or personal items in the press—I address this letter to my anonymous friend:

Dear Child of suffering, son of God: It is Friday night, cold and wet and rainy. Darby O'Gill, my dog, slumbers at my feet. Tonight I need symphonies as a background to comfort worries; instead I have only puppy snores and memories of your letters; composed on other Friday evenings when your best entertainment was to write sad words to an unknown priest. Do you remember when you were a child first awakening to an awareness of people? Everyone, you thought (if your mind was like mine), came in different stages of being big folks or little folks: roughly, they were old, middle-aged, young, and your age. Grandparents were old people, and always had been; therefore, they were perishable, but you preferred not to think about that. Aunts were middle-aged spinsters confirmed in prudence who could never have splashed through mud puddles or hated winter underwear; they would, predictably, always remain tacky, generous, and vaguely forty. Only the child had birthdays that involved growing up and change; everyone else would remain stuck in the same gutter of age. But after a cycle of years, you learned the first sad lesson of time: when you were growing up, the young had become middle-aged; the middle-aged had become old (maiden aunts have here no lasting city), and the old had shuffled off to God in bedroom slippers.

"Change and decay—in all around I see," we cheerfully sang in my days as a choirboy. Another stanza should have taught us this lesson: it is not only beauty and life that disappear in the cycle of time. Pain too passes, along with heartbreak, fear, and sickness. In a world doomed to fragility, death itself shall someday die. Even your longest Friday faces the dawn of tomorrow. Daybreak can come at any moment, now as in eternity, when all the lights and shadows of pain and joy will fall into a single pattern of love at the feet of the Superstar.

Recently, a friend of mine called my attention to an extraordinary sight: from the rear door of Kennan Hall, we looked up at the statute of Our Lady Mother poised against the gray slate of a storm-threatened sky. Never, it seemed to me, had that compassionate image looked more golden. Then—oh, shock, oh, grief—I noted for the first time ever that on that Tiffany-plated head, where diadems should have rested, there was a lightning rod: a symbol of fear on a symbol of hope. Our Lady of the Immaculate Protection, herself protected. In the kingdom of a lonely heaven, where suffering is the first law of life, even its Queen must fear the doom of fire tumbling from the skies; and all of us, in Merton's phrase, are the brothers of God learning to know the Christ of the burnt men.

The God lonely enough to permit suffering is neither cruel nor indifferent. The rumor that He dotes upon us like a hen nesting its chicks is not, despite evidence to the contrary, just a tale of the myth-makers. People needing to love one another is what you're left with when you can't find God, who brooks alone, or when you shrink from Him because of the pain. Loving one another, and being loved, is what He commanded us to do; it is a condition qualifying us for the fellowship of saints caught into joy in the Everlasting Arms: "A man who does not love the brother that he can see cannot love God whom he has never seen."

Unknown friend, all love, without exception, is a fulfillment of God's command. *All* love—puppy love, parent's love, sexual love, celibate love, saint's love, sinner's love, married love, courting love—all of it, if it is love, is an exercise of holy precepts, and is from the lifestream of the Trinity. Love, to achieve maturity, constantly needs self-discipline and restraint; lovers must always guard themselves against love's parody, chiefly notable for its self-indulgence.

As long as you live with your heart in a hermitage, in flight from passion, you will never find healing. Like every other soul, you've got to take the risk of loving. Within the context of that experience, learn the cost of discipleship in the company of Christ who taught us that love makes its journey with a cross on its back.

There are no easy roads to one's personal destiny in the Kingdom of the Lonely God.

In 1967, I was assigned for the summer to a church in upper Manhattan, about two blocks from the George Washington Bridge. It was a parish in transition: part Irish ghetto, part Spanish enclave, with a steadily growing number of immigrants from Puerto Rico and the Dominican Republic. The rectory was surrounded by bodegas, carnicerias, shamrock saloons, and tenement houses. One stepped immediately out of the front door, onto a stoop, into a constantly passing sidewalk parade of handsome, dark-eyed children, young adult blacks, and thick-brogued harps fifty years over from the

Galway coast. Among the Spanish folk of the neighborhood, I was commonly known as El Gordo, "The Fat One."

On the morning of July 16, I was awakened, as the priest on duty, by the police. There was a jumper over at the bridge, they said, threatening suicide. Would the Father please come to help argue with the guy?

It was the kind of situation that a seminarian dreams of. Young astronauts anticipate the moment they will land among galaxies never touched by visits from the moon; young actors look forward to the evening they will star as Lear. Novices in religion except their fulfillment in scenes of redemptive drama at spots quite remote from the teas in the rectory parlor. However, I never expected to be invited to shinny up the cables of my own mighty bridge in a ministry to some soul, perhaps an anguished atheist, who might be awaiting salvation from his perch among the pylons of the George Washington.

So on the morning of July 16 it was El Gordo—spiritually booted and spurred and ready to ride—to the rescue. In a matter of minutes, with buttons loose and zippers unattended, I appeared, like the Holy Name Society's Don Quixote, among the cops on the bridge.

Among the roar of cars that pass from Jersey to New York in the early morning, El Gordo was more of a roadblock perilous to traffic than he was a comfort to the perishing. He came closer to going home with his tail, quite literally, in his hands than he did to gathering stars for his crown of glory. But as a groovy place for the apostolate, that bride-setting was superior to every fantasy known to seminarians but the blonde-one-the-skyscraper scenes in the final moments of *King Kong*.

A slim youth, about twenty, balanced himself like a tightrope walker on the outer rail of the sidewalk. Sporadically, he shouted warnings to a group of twenty policemen to keep their distance; otherwise, he said, he would jump. Behind him, the spires of midtown Manhattan were silhouetted against the pink flush of the morning sky. Underneath, the waters of the majestic Hudson swept outward to the sea. Overhead was all the grace, poetry, and technical mystery that cling to the superstructure of a mighty bridge as part of its essential miracle. It was a scene worthy of the death of kings, but it seemed intolerable that one skinny kid should perish in the glory of that dawn.

For an hour and a half, stratagems of rescue were plotted and defeated. Finally, in a superbly timed move, the boy was distracted into an exchange of insults with a group of cops on his right; instantly, another group of cops moved in to grab him from the left. I have seen the New York police in action in a number of emergency situations; I have seen the Tactical Police Force, white-helmeted, tough, with clubs in their hands, disperse a crowd of a thousand people from a city park. I had not known that cops could be so gentle as they were with that boy whom they had to wrestle to the ground and handcuff until his delivery at Bellevue Hospital. A priest could not touch the sacrament with greater reverence than the way the police handled that struggling body, seemingly so anxious to fling itself into the garbage of a modern river.

For El Gordo, that fat, comic creature who stumbled flatfootedly among the rescue squad, as big as the rest of the assembled crowd and nearly as broad as the bridge, it was not an hour of charismatic service, and he didn't even care. A twenty-your-old youngster had wanted to die, and all the resources of the Unreal City had organized against his death wish; ambulances, patrol cars, fire boats down on the river, and a small army of cops. The boy's problem was this: he had quarreled with his only friend, another fellow of twenty, and he felt there was no one else in the world who loved him enough to make life worth living. El Gordo had participated as an observer in one of the eight million stories of the Naked City; it was wretched, pathetic, and deviant, and it sent him, still unbuttoned and non-zippered, home to his rectory in tears. He went back to his church, a fat man touched by loneliness, about to say early Mass for lonely people in a lonely city, where alienated brothers live heaped together as joyless as ants.

Often Notre Dame seems like a suburb of the Unreal City, sharing with it the contemporary paradox of the lonely crowd. The campus seems very much a part of an idiot world, overcrowded enough to burst the seams of the stratosphere, where there is never enough human warmth to quiet all the hearts wretched with isolation, and restless minds constantly fret themselves into dilemmas of drink, drugs, breakdown, and rage that cries against heaven. Among current suicides, even youngsters in the grade schools, psychiatrists tell us, are destroying themselves as an alternative to belonging to no one as a cherished lamb-child. In college dorms students are running into situations where all the signs seem to read: "Lamb-children in need of cherishing should not apply here."

El Gordo eventually got to meet the boy from the bridge. The encounter occurred last summer in a New York funeral parlor. Death was due to an over-use of narcotics, the undertaker said. The body had gone several days undiscovered in a shabby room off Riverside Drive. It was another couple of days before any family could be found who would claim the body. But, the undertaker said, that is not an uncommon situation, these days, in the morgues of the Unreal City.

After the six days of Creation, according to Genesis, God was weary from His chores of nailing down the firmament. His back ached from shaping whale bumps and elephants, and His fingers were all nicks and cuts from the snap of shark teeth and punctures from the rose thorn. For an entire Sunday, He slept, waking only for a worship service where He hummed the Doxology to Himself, with the Father taking the bass part, and the Son and the Spirit joining in as first and second tenors.

When, late Sunday afternoon, He looked again at His new-made world and saw that suffering and desolation had entered it, He turned His head and wept. He brooded alone in sorrow until all the heavens were swallowed up in celestial midnight; and when the morning star exploded into atoms in its efforts to herald the dawn (God thought to Himself, "It little matters"), Omnipotence once again donned His overalls and set to work.

He lifted all living creatures made in His image onto the palm of His hand: old men and little babies, girls ready to marry and grandmothers about to die, young fathers and their children, presidents and kings and future popes. He saw every one of them flawed with selfishness and disease, and all were marked for death.

So God blew fire upon all the creatures made in His image, and the breath of immortality (new-damaged by sin), which was His gift on the sixth day of Creation, returned like a dove winging homeward, to his place in the Father's heart; and humanity lay in dust upon the hands of its Creator. God let the dust sift through his fingers onto the earth from which it had come. Then, tapping gently, He set the world to rocking, so that in every land, on every continent, the earth opened up with quakes to reclaim the once glorious clay. Every other living creature—cattle, reptiles, and wild animals—perished with terror on that day the earth trembled. At the end of the first day of the Uncreation, every animal had been reclaimed by the womb out of which it had been delivered.

God looked at His destruction and saw that it was sad.

On the second day, God's eye scanned the heavens in search of each bird in the air, whether great or tiny, and He commanded that the flutter should slip out of its wings. He searched the woodlands and house-eaves and the parks where the nightingales loved to sing to lovers; and hushing all melodies, He watched until the final sparrow had fallen in its flight. Wading into the ocean, He broke the spin of the great behemoth like the teeth of a comb. He sent terrible monsters after prey in the deepest part of the sea, where He crushed them by scooping all the weight of the waters onto their backs. He commanded that the greater fish should swallow the smaller; and with lightning bolts as harpoons, he slaughtered the mighty whales until He grew sick at the sight of blood. When destruction was everywhere in the water, He commanded that the sea should change the carcasses into the elements from which the coral reefs are formed. The ocean was dead as though God had cursed it, and its billows rolled onto the shore in tides of death.

On the third day, God snuffed the light from the sun and moon. Daylight failed forever, and there were no more seasons or years. He shook the stars out of the firmament, and they fell like meteors into the dead sea, where, ashamed of their lost glory, they hid among the watery graves of drowned sailors.

On the fourth day, God sent storms and tempests to beat down the forests, the gardens, the wheat fields, and the jungles. He raged at the mossy violet and Lebanon cedars with hailstones and hoar frost and chills borne on winds from the heart of a glacier. Now nothing at all lived on the face of the earth, and God ground the mountains into dust for the burial rites of the garden where his Eden had bloomed. Then He cracked the crossbeams of the firmament, and the rains fell from a dark and empty sky, and the ocean flooded the whole earth with its death tide until finally, under the merciless heaven, there was only the great, gray stretch of brackish water.

On the fifth day, the ocean and the sky collided; the vault separating the rain clouds from sea water collapsed, and the heavens were altogether destroyed. God mourned the loss of heaven where His feet had danced on the second morning of the creation of the world.

On the sixth day, God commanded that the light should cease. The earth was without form and void, with darkness over the face of the abyss, and a mighty wind swept over the surface of the waters.

On the seventh day, God—Father, Son, and Holy Spirit—slept alone . . . and, like lots of old people not having much to get up for anymore, He lay there dreaming of a lost paradise . . . until finally, out of grief, He touched His heart to hush the beating.

In the end, there was nothing.

Unicorns and whales—little figures which I have collected as symbols of the mystery and whimsy of God's Kingdom. The whales—stylized in metal, wood, or bone—heavy, ponderous substances shaped into wave-slapping fin and sea-pounding head: playful, death-bearing mammals whose power reveals the cosmic indifference of mere Omnipotence. The unicorn—light-bearing glass shaped into the postures of grace—framed in fragility, sinewed the sun: the emblem of sexual love, the medieval figure for Christ.

Today, at Mass, a young man named John gave me the news: he had just mailed back his draft card, and it was his twenty-first birthday.

On a single shelf of my bookcase they are collected, the unicorns and the whales, together like the lights and shadows in the face of God. God was in His sterner mood, I think, when He created the whale to swim the fierce seas creatured with beauty and overkill. Quite different from the saga of smashed-in boats and splintered limbs are the slightly erotic adventures of a questing unicorn.

According to the bestiaries, the unicorn is a single-horned beast that grows starry-eyed and weak-kneed with joy at the first footfall of the virgin maiden on the garden path. According to the best ancient sources, a unicorn is at its happiest when it is allowed to rescue a virgin maiden from the inconvenience of being lashed to a tree by her demon lover. In an age when the woods were filled with virgin maidenhood pinioned to the shrubbery, unicorns apparently massed themselves into rescue packs and roamed the thicket like St. Bernards crossing the Alps.

Today, alas, the one-horned beast is seen no more in the land, and who weeps now for the unicorn? Only virgin maidens, it is to be feared; if they too should become extinct, we should all have cause for mourning.

In the bestiaries, Christ was seen, spiritually, as the Unicorn alluded to in the *Benedictus*: "He has raised up a horn of salvation for us in the house of his servant David." The image of the horn is heraldic rather than erotic; but Christ is traditionally described under the images of a young, sensuous lover, as is evident in the application to Him of the Bridegroom's lyrics in the Song of Songs.

It is as a Christ-image, a Savior-figure into which has been blended the roles of lover and deliverer of innocence, that I love the unicorn best. Once at the Urchins' Mass I tried to explain passiontide as the season of the breaking of the unicorn. First, I showed the children a one-horned, milk-white little figure that had suffered from a fall: a leg was broken, and the horn had disappeared entirely. Then I showed them another unicorn, a twin to the first; he was whole and intact and full of beauty. On Easter, I explained, the brokenness in christ will be healed; like the unicorn, He will be renewed in loveliness, and full of beauty also. Unfortunately, afterward, I left the unfallen figure on a table, out of harm's way, to remind us of the promise of Resurrection. There a child, full of wonder and love, approached the fragile creature too closely; in a moment, it too lay smashed on the floor, for it was indeed the season of the breaking of the unicorn.

Also at Mass today was a boy named Jim. Sometimes, when I see him in church, I think of that night nearly a year ago when that same face looked up at me from a bed in the emergency room at St. Joseph's Hospital. It was a night memorable for the bodies broken in the traffic of Notre Dame Avenue.

A few days later, a new unicorn came to live on my shelf. With him was a note: "You see, Father, he was broken—but just as it was we who broke him, it's also we who can put him together by sharing him with each other . . ."

Near the entrance of the campus, close to a spot where the Virgin Mother is a prisoner of the midnight shadows, there was, on that night of accidents, the impact of speeding steel on living flesh, and Mark lay dead on the street.

John and Mark and Jim, full of light and grace, the children of Omnipotence, framed in fragility, sinewed with sun . . . Mark and Jim and John, the unicorn as broken, as mended, as deliverer of innocence yet unfallen from the hand of life . . . Mark and John and Jim, representatives of a generation created in beauty and strength, but hopefully not as the playthings of whimsy . . .

O God, who made the whale for power and the glass to give light, send forth Your children, metaphored in the myth of the gentle beast, not to face the hour of their breaking, but to share in the season of mending for a world that lies shattered like a fallen unicorn at Thy clumsy, lonely feet.